14213

DATE DUE

I Believe in Youth, Christ
Believes in Youth

DEMCO

I BELIEVE IN YOUTH
CHRIST BELIEVES IN YOUTH

I Believe in Youth,

Christ Believes in Youth

To the Young People of the World

POPE JOHN PAUL II

*Compiled and Indexed by the
Daughters of St. Paul*

ST. PAUL EDITIONS

Reprinted with permission from *L'Osservatore Romano,* English Edition.

ISBN   0-8198-3602-8 cloth
         0-8198-3603-6 paper

CREDITS:
DSP—cover
Felici—56, 62, 65, 71, 82,
        93, 101, 112, 128, 137,
        146, 178, 184, 209, 221,
        223, 275
A. Mari—242, 292
John Murray—53
Wide World Photos—17, 77, 155,
        265
Virginia Broderick, 279

Printed in U.S.A. by the Daughters of St. Paul
50 St. Paul's Ave., Boston, MA 02130

The Daughters of St. Paul are an international
congregation of religious women serving the Church
with the communications media.

Contents

You Are My Most Precious Treasure!

Introduction

The luminous figure of Jesus Christ, our Savior and Redeemer, is the central point of the life of Pope John Paul II and of these warm talks he addresses to youth.

Our Holy Father's words spring from a heart and life totally anchored in the hope and love of the Son of God, the Redeemer of mankind.

Pope John Paul II is fully confident in this hope. His security and peace are evident in his words and life and act as an electrifying charge that revivifies all who see him, hear him or read his messages.

I Believe in Youth, Christ Believes in Youth is a volume that breathes hope, confidence, joy and challenges. The young and all who deal with them in any way will find in these pages reassuring direction and secure strength for life.

Jesus and His Gospel are presented as the source and goal of all desires and activities. Personality, careers, states in life, pain and sorrow, joys and successes—all converge in the attractive Person of Jesus Christ.

The young will feel that they are indeed loved and trusted, and that they are capable of valiant responses to this love and trust.

I Believe in Youth, Christ Believes in Youth is this "electrical charge" of confidence needed by our young people, and, indeed, by all persons today.

You Are My Most Precious Treasure!

On October 13, 1979, the Holy Father presided over a Eucharistic con-celebration for 82 young seminarians of the Major Seminary of Rome and delivered the following homily.

Beloved clerics of the Roman Seminary!

You can imagine with what affection and trepidation I celebrate holy Mass this evening with you and for you, at the end of your spiritual exercises and at the beginning of the new academic year!

You are, in fact, my seminarians, pupils of the seminary of my diocese, Rome, which the Lord entrusted to me when He made provision for my election as Sovereign Pontiff, and I, as already in Krakow and like every other bishop, consider you my most precious treasure, which has its place within my heart and my concerns. Even though, owing to the care and service of the universal Church, I must, as my Predecessors always did, delegate a large part of the direct ministry to the Cardinal Vicar, the Viceregent, and the auxiliary bishops, you are, however, particularly present in my daily prayer and fatherly concern.

We are gathered here round the altar to offer the Lord the holy Eucharistic Sacrifice and to seal concretely the resolutions for a holy and committed life, which you have certainly formulated in these days of silence and reflection.

While I thank you warmly for your goodwill and express to you my deep joy at this meeting, such a significant one, I also wish to suggest to you some indications that are appropriate at this particular moment.

Maintain constant and fervent your sense of joy in the truth you know.

It is really impressive to think that one possesses truth, that is, to know the meaning of human life, the significance of history and of the whole universe, the reason for existence, which is unfolded between peaks of scientific achievements and abysses of misery and grief.

The truth is God, Creator, Redeemer and Rewarder; the truth is Christ, who defined Himself precisely the "way, the truth, the life, light, love, salvation"; the truth is the Church, willed and founded by Him to transmit His Word in full and the means of salvation! And you possess, you enjoy all this admirable heritage!

How many young people do not possess the truth, and drift along without a "reason why"; how many, unfortunately, after empty and exhausting searches, disappointed and embittered, have given and still give themselves up to despair! And how many have succeeded in reaching the truth only after years of tormented questioning and painful experiences!

Just think, for example, of St. Augustine's dramatic path to arrive at the light of truth and at the peace of regained innocence! What a sigh he heaved when at last he arrived at the light! And he exclaimed with nostalgia: *"Sero Te amavi!"* ("Late have I loved You!")

Just think of the effort the famous Cardinal Newman had to make to arrive with the force of logic at Catholicism! What a long and painful spiritual agony!

In this way we could recall so many other eminent figures, past and recent, who had to fight hard to reach the truth.

Well, they arrived where you already are. You, in fact, possess truth, the whole, luminous and consoling truth! How many people envy your situation!

Learn, therefore, how to enjoy truth, as St. Thomas says; learn how to live by the truth and in the truth. Learn how to study more deeply and understand more and more, and better and better, truth in all its aspects and in all its requirements: philosophical, theological, scientific, juridical and social, for your own deep requirements and to be "witnesses to truth" everywhere.

You have time, books and qualified teachers in order to become intensely dedicated to the truth and then be able, one day, to communicate it with certainty and capability: Do not waste time. Above all do not venture into mined and dangerous fields, do not be over confident and presumptuous, because it is easy to fall into confusion and be overcome by pride. Learn how to be sensitive and docile, in order not to waste or spoil the immensely precious gift that you possess.

Recognize your responsibility.

Reflect on your "identity": You have been called, elected by Jesus Himself, the Divine Master, the Pastor and Savior of our souls, the Redeemer of man. He has chosen you, in a mysterious but real way, to make you saviors with Him and like Him; He wants to change you into Himself, to entrust to you His own divine powers.... One day you will have to act *in persona Christi!*

Therefore, you are not like other youths, who have before them only the normal aims of a career, social position, marriage, earthly satisfactions, even though with Christian and even apostolic ideals.

You are different, because you are called to the priesthood.

And so you must base your life on a type of formation and responsibility that is eminently one of apostolate and witness.

To young people gathered in Galway, Ireland, I said recently: "Yes, Christ calls you, but He calls you in truth. His call is demanding, because He invites you to let yourselves be 'captured' by Him completely, so that your whole lives will be seen in a different light" (September 30, 1979).

If this holds good for the young, how much more so for you, beloved seminarians! Let yourselves be seized by Jesus and try to live just for Him!

I wish to confide in you, too, what I said to Irish seminarians at Maynooth: "The Word of God is the great treasure of your lives.... God counts on you, He makes His plans, in a way, depend on your free collaboration, on the oblation of your lives, and on the generosity with which you follow the inspirations of the Holy Spirit in the depths of your hearts." And again: "You are preparing for the total giving of yourselves to Christ and to service of His kingdom. You bring to Christ the gift of your youthful enthusiasm and vitality. In you Christ is eternally youthful; and through you He gives youth to the Church. Do not disappoint Him. Do not disappoint the people who are waiting for you to bring Christ to them.... Christ looks on you and loves you" (October 1, 1979).

Finally: keep alive your sense of commitment.

You wish to become priests, or at least you wish to discover if you are really called. And so the question is a serious one, because it is necessary to prepare thoroughly, with clear intentions and an austere formation. The world looks to the priest, because it looks to Jesus! No one can see

Christ; but everyone sees the priest, and through him they wish to catch a glimpse of the Lord! Immense is the grandeur and dignity of the priest, who has rightly been called *alter Christus!*

Therefore, do not waste time! Constant and unflagging commitment in your formation is, in fact, necessary:

—commitment in spiritual formation;

—commitment in intellectual and cultural formation;

—commitment in ascetic formation, through the habit of order, poverty, sacrifice, mortification, control of one's desires, recalling the ever valid admonition in the *Imitation of Christ: "Tantum proficies quantum tibi ipsi vim intuleris."* (Your progress will be in proportion to the self-mastery you impose on yourself. Bk. I, ch. XXIV, no. 11)

I told the seminarians of Philadelphia, after quoting *Optatam totius* (no. 11), that the seminary must provide a wholesome discipline to prepare for consecrated service: "When discipline is properly exercised, it can create an atmosphere of recollection which enables the seminarian to develop interiorly those attitudes which are so desirable in a priest, such as joyful obedience, generosity and self-sacrifice" (October 3, 1979).

—commitment in the formation of one's character. A good character is a real treasure in life. Sometimes priests of excellent virtue and zeal drastically reduce the efficacy of their ministry because of their impatient, unfriendly temperament and lack of balance. It is necessary, therefore, to form for oneself a good, open, understanding, patient character; and sincere and methodical spiritual direction certainly helps to do so;

—commitment in social formation, becoming acquainted with the psychology of the various classes and their requirements, acquiring various possibilities of entering into communication, learning too to be self-sufficient for so many necessities of life.

Beloved seminarians!

May the Lord help you and accompany you every day of this new year of study and formation.

To you, too, as at the Maynooth meeting, I say: "This is a wonderful time in the history of the Church. This is a wonderful time to be a priest, to be a religious, to be a missionary for Christ. Rejoice in the Lord always. Rejoice in your vocation" (October 1, 1979).

To succeed in your intention, entrust yourselves to the Blessed Virgin always, but especially in moments of difficulty and darkness. "From Mary we learn to surrender to God's will in all things. From Mary we learn to trust even when all hope seems gone. From Mary we learn to love Christ, her Son and the Son of God.... Learn from her to be always faithful, to trust that God's Word to you will be fulfilled, and that nothing is impossible with God" (Address in St. Matthew's Cathedral, Washington, October 6, 1979).

And may my blessing, which I impart with deep affection to you, to your superiors and teachers, and to all those dear to you, also be propitious for you.

"Evangelization Needs the Generous Energies of Youth"

On October 20, 1979, the eve of World Mission Sunday, 20,000 of the faithful, for the most part young people, took part in a vigil in the Duomo of Milan. The vigil concluded with a solemn concelebrated Mass presided over by Cardinal Colombo, Archbishop of Milan, who presented crucifixes to eighteen new missionaries. To the young people who took part in the vigil, John Paul II sent the following message by radio.

I am happy to address the large numbers of young people, gathered in Milan Cathedral together with the Cardinal Archbishop Giovanni Colombo for a missionary vigil, on the occasion of World Mission Sunday.

Beloved young people, I greet you all with the joy of one who knows he has in you the guarantee of a Church which is always young, and which, in the name of Christ, man's Redeemer, wishes to put her own fresh and generous energies in the service of the serious spiritual and material needs of the modern world. From the day of the first Pentecost, the Christian community has always been, by its very nature, a missionary one, that is, striving to emerge from its own frontiers to propose and give to all men "the message of this salvation" (Acts 13:26), "that they may have life and have it abundantly" (Jn. 10:10).

You, too, dear young people, and not only those among you who receive the crucifix from the hands of the Archbishop this evening, are called by the Lord to continue this admirable story of love and giving, of facts and not just words. Only by experiencing it could you discover the exalting truth of Jesus' words: "Whoever loses his life for my sake and the gospel's will save it" (Mk. 8:35). Therefore, I beseech the Lord that your prayers and your commitment will yield fruit not only for the missionary requirements of the Church, but also for yourselves, as protagonists in the first person of the orders left us by Jesus, before He ascended to the Father (cf. Mt. 28:19). And may my apostolic blessing be for you a fatherly stimulus for a wholly missionary life, as well as a sure sign of my benevolence.

Tremendous Ideals Are in Front of You

Because of the Pope's visit to Pompeii on October 21, 1979, the Mass for World Mission Sunday was celebrated by the Holy Father in St. Peter's on Saturday evening, October 20. Many thousands were present at the Mass and the liturgical singing was led by a choir formed by the youth movement "Communion and Liberation."

After the Gospel reading which was taken from St. Mark, Pope John Paul preached the following homily.

Beloved brothers and sisters in the Lord!

Beloved young people!

With great, deep joy I preside over the Eucharistic liturgy, on this eve of "World Mission Sunday," to meet you all, faithful of the diocese of Rome. In this way I feel more closely linked, not only with all the dioceses in the world on this important and significant occasion, but particularly with the men and women missionaries who, scattered in the various parts of the world, joyfully and laboriously proclaim the Gospel of salvation to men.

Yes, dear friends, this is a very important occasion for your spiritual life and for our diocese. Here in the center of Christianity, in this Vatican Basilica, we hear the echoes of the universal Church, we perceive the needs of all peoples, we share the anxieties of all those who, with indefatigable ardor, walk in the name of Christ, bear witness, proclaim, convert, baptize and found new Christian communities.

Let us meditate briefly, and seek together, following the readings of the liturgy, the motivation, the condition and the strategy of the Church's missionary activity.

What is the first and ultimate motivation of this work?

Here is the first question. And the answer is a simple and peremptory one: the Church is missionary by the express will of God.

Jesus often speaks to the Apostles of their task, their mission, the reason for their choice: "You did not choose me, but I chose you and appointed you that you should go and bear fruit and that your fruit should abide" (Jn. 15:16).

Before ascending to heaven, Jesus gives the Apostles, and through them the whole Church, the mission of evangelizing, in an official and decisive way: "Go into all the world and preach the gospel to the whole creation" (Mk. 16:15). And the evangelist notes: "And they went forth and preached everywhere" (Mk. 16:20).

From that time the Apostles and disciples of Christ began to travel over the roads of the earth, to overcome hardships and weariness, to meet gentiles and tribes, peoples and nations, to suffer to the extent of giving their lives; in order to proclaim the Gospel, because it is the will of God; and with regard to God the only decision is that of obedience and love.

St. Paul wrote to his disciple Timothy: "God desires all men to be saved and to come to the knowledge of the truth" (1 Tm. 2:4).

The truth that saves is only Jesus Christ, the Redeemer, the Mediator between God and men, the one and definitive Revealer of man's supernatural destiny. Jesus gave the Church the mission of proclaiming the Gospel; every Christian takes part in this mission. Every Christian is a missionary by his very nature. Paul VI, of venerated memory, wrote in the Apostolic Exhortation *Evangelii nuntiandi:*

"The presentation of the Gospel message is not an optional contribution for the Church. It is the duty incumbent on her by the command of the Lord Jesus, so that people can believe and be saved. This message is indeed necessary. It is unique. It cannot be replaced. It does not permit either indifference, syncretism or accommodation. It is a question of people's salvation. It is the beauty of the Revelation that it represents. It brings with it a wisdom that is not of this world. It is able to stir up by itself faith—faith that rests on the power of God. It is truth. It merits having the apostle consecrate to it all his time and all his energies, and to sacrifice for it, if necessary, his own life" (no. 5). "Evangelizing is, in fact, the grace and vocation proper to the Church, her deepest identity. She exists in order to evangelize" (no. 14).

It is sometimes affirmed that it is not possible to impose the Gospel, that it is not possible to violate religious liberty, that it is, in fact, useless and illusory to proclaim the Gospel to those who already belong to Christ in an anonymous way owing to uprightness of heart. Paul VI already replied clearly as follows: "It would certainly be an error to impose something on the consciences of our brethren. But to propose to their consciences the truth of the Gospel and salvation in Jesus Christ, with complete clarity and with a total respect for the free options which it presents, far from being an attack on religious liberty, is fully to respect that liberty, which is offered the choice of a way that even non-believers consider noble and uplifting.... The respectful presentation of Christ and His Kingdom is more than the evangelizer's right; it is his duty. It is likewise the right of his fellowmen to receive from him the proclamation of the Good News of salvation" (EN, 80).

These are very serious words, but above all illuminating and encouraging, which state clearly once more what is God's positive will and our responsibility as Christians.

But let us ask ourselves a second question: What is the essential condition for missionary work? It is unity in doctrine.

Before leaving this world, Jesus prayed as follows: "I do not pray for these only, but also for those who believe in me through their word, that they may all be one; even as you, Father, are in me, and I in you, that they also may be in us, so that the world may believe that you have sent me" (Jn. 17:20-21).

St. Paul wrote anxiously to his disciple Timothy: "There is one God, and there is one mediator between God and men, the man Christ Jesus, who gave himself as a ransom for all" (1 Tm. 2:5-6).

In fact, if unity in faith is lacking, who and what is proclaimed? How is it possible to be credible, especially when the doctrine is so mysterious and the morality so demanding? Differences and doctrinal conflicts create only confusion and finally disappointment. In such an essential and delicate matter as the content of the Gospel, it is not possible to be overconfident, or superficial, or possibilist, inventing theories and setting forth hypotheses. Evangelization must have, as its characteristic, unity in faith and in discipline, and therefore love of truth.

Let us meditate on the well-balanced and profound words of Paul VI: "Every evangelizer is expected to have a reverence for truth, especially since the truth that he studies and communicates is none other than revealed truth and hence, more than any other, a sharing in the first truth which is God Himself. The preacher of the Gospel will, therefore, be a person who even at the price of personal renunciation and suffering always seeks the truth that he must transmit to others. He never betrays or hides truth out of a desire to please men, in order to astonish or to shock, nor for the sake of originality or a desire to make an impression. He does not refuse truth. He does not obscure revealed truth by being too idle to search for it, or for the sake of his own comfort, or out of fear. He does not neglect to study it. He serves it generously, without making it serve him" *(EN,* no. 78).

Let us thank Paul VI for these clear indications, and at the same time let us pray fervently that everyone will study, know and proclaim the truth and only the truth, docile to the authentic Magisterium of the Church, because certainty and clarity are the indispensable qualities of evangelization.

Finally, here is the last question: What is the strategy of missionary work? For this question, too, the answer is a simple one: love!

The only and indispensable strategy for missionary work is precisely deep, personal, convinced, ardent love of Jesus Christ!

Let us recall the joyful exclamation, of St. Theresa of Lisieux: "My vocation is love!... In the heart of the Church, my Mother, I will be love...and so I will be everything!" (Man. B.)

It must be so for us, too!

—Love is intrepid and courageous: Jesus is still unknown to three-quarters of mankind! The Church, therefore, needs so many willing missionaries, men and women, to proclaim the Gospel! You boys and girls, be attentive to the ·voice of God calling! Stupendous ideals of charity, generosity and dedication are in front of you and call upon you! Life is noble and great only to the extent that it is given! Be fearless! Supreme joy lies in love without claims, in the pure giving of charity to brothers!

—Love is docile and confident in the action of "grace." It is the Holy Spirit that penetrates souls and transforms peoples. The difficulties are always immense, and particularly today the faithful themselves, involved in present-day history, are tempted by atheism, secularism, moral autonomy. Absolute confidence in the work of the Holy Spirit is, therefore, necessary *(EN,* no. 75). Therefore, the Christian in his missionary work is patient and joyful, even if he has to sow in tears, accepting the cross and maintaining the spirit of the beatitudes.

—Finally, love is ingenious and constant, exercising itself in the various types of missionary apostolate: the apostolate of example, of prayer, of suffering, of charity, taking advantage of all the initiatives and means proposed by the Pontifical Mission Aid Societies, so well-deserving and so active in Rome and in all the dioceses.

I cannot, however, forget some actual situations which make the missionary duty of the whole Church, and of all of us who form her, more compelling today. There are various forms of anti-evangelization in progress which seek to oppose radically the message of Christ: the elimination of all transcendence and of all responsibility for the afterlife; ethical autonomy released from every natural and revealed moral law; hedonism considered as the one, satisfying system of life; and, in so many Christians, a weakening of spiritual fervor, a giving way to a worldly outlook, a gradual acceptance of the erroneous opinions of laicism and social and political immanentism.

Let us always keep in mind St. Paul's cry: "Caritas Christi urget nos!" "The love of Christ impels us!" (2 Cor. 5:14)

The Apostle's ardent exclamation takes on particular eloquence and causes particular solicitude in our times. It is the missionary imperative that must move all Christians, dioceses, parishes and the various communities. Love of Christ urges us to bear witness, to announce, to proclaim the Good News, to everyone and in spite of everything!

Precisely in these times you must be witnesses and missionaries of truth: Do not be afraid! Love of Christ must drive you to be strong and resolute, because "if God is for us, who is against us?" (Rom. 8:31) No one, in fact, can "separate us from the love of Christ" (Rom. 8:35).

But we must turn our attention also to those territories and nations of the world where, unfortunately, the Gospel cannot be preached, where the missionary activity of the Church is forbidden. The Church wishes to proclaim only the joy of divine fatherhood, the consolation of redemption carried out by Christ, the brotherhood of all men! Missionaries wish only to proclaim true and just peace, the peace of love of Christ and in Christ, our Brother and Savior. Whole peoples are waiting for the living water of truth and grace and are thirsty for it! Let us pray that the Word of God may pass freely and swiftly (Ps. 147:15) to all peoples on earth.

For this reason the missionary Church needs, in the first place, missionary souls in prayer: Let us be close to evangelizers with our prayer! Especially for the missions we must always pray, tirelessly. Let us pray in the first place by means of the Holy Mass, joining in Christ's sacrifice for the salvation of all men: May the Eucharist keep the faith of Christians firm and fervent!

But let us pray also with constancy and confidence to the Blessed Virgin, the Queen of the Missions, that she may make the faithful feel ever more deeply concerned for evangelization and responsibility for the proclamation of the Gospel. Let us pray to her in particular with the recitation of the holy rosary, to reach in this way, and help those who are laboring amid difficulties and hardships, to make Jesus known and loved!

Mary, who was present on the day of Pentecost at the beginning of the life of the Church with the Apostles, disciples and pious women, always remains present in the Church, she, the first woman missionary, Mother and support of all those who proclaim the Gospel!

"The Pope Loves You Very Much"

On October 21, 1979, the Holy Father visited the Basilica of Our Lady of the Rosary of Pompeii. After kneeling in prayer before a picture of the Madonna, the Holy Father spoke to the bishops, priests, religious, and faithful gathered there. The following is an excerpt from his address.

To you, boys and girls, who serenely pass your childhood close to the Blessed Virgin, I address my affectionate and fatherly greeting. You know how much Jesus loves children! Fascinated by His word and His personality, they manifested their affection exuberantly; and Jesus wanted to be with the children. He did not allow the Apostles to send them away: "Let the children come to me, and do not hinder them; for to such belongs the kingdom of God" (Lk. 18:16). The Pope too, like Jesus, loves you very much, entrusts himself to your prayers, and today, at this meeting, says to you: Always be faithful and sincere friends of Jesus; study His example, His life, His teaching, contained in the Gospel. But to be faithful and sincere friends of Jesus means following Him, and putting into practice, every day, what He said. Then you will be really happy, for you will be exemplary Christians and good citizens.

"Draw Example and Comfort from the Saints"

During the general audience of October 31, 1979, the Holy Father spoke a special word to the young people present.

A particularly affectionate greeting goes to all the young, who have flocked here in large numbers, today also, to gladden this general audience. Beloved young people, I thank you warmly for this significant presence of yours, a sign of donation to Christ, and of communion with His Vicar on earth. Your generous aspirations of spirit always give me such joy. As the Church celebrates the feast of All Saints' Day tomorrow, I call upon you, dear young people, to turn your thought to the indefectible realities, the reason for our hope, and to draw example and comfort from those who followed the Lord with heroic adherence, and now wish to help us to travel courageously along the same way of salvation. I impart a special blessing to you all.

Walking Towards Heaven

On November 1, 1979, at 9 a.m., John Paul II greeted from the window of his private study participants in the "First Ecological March" through the streets of the city organized by the Roman company "Radiotaxi" with the collaboration of the councillors for Sport and Culture of the City Council. Children and adults took part in the march from St. Peter's Square to Siena Square.

The Holy Father addressed them as follows.

Beloved in Christ!

The Roman company "Radiotaxi," with the collaboration of the councillors for Sport and Culture of the City Council of Rome, has organized this "First Ecological March" along the streets of our city, and has wished to have the Pope's greeting. I thank you warmly for your respect, and I willingly extend my best wishes to everyone.

May the march you are about to begin, through the magnificent streets of the capital, make you feel more and more united, good and understanding, so that peace, charity, respect and brotherly aid may always reign among you, citizens of Rome.

Since your march falls precisely today, November 1, All Saints' Day, I wish you all the power to feel deeply the joy that springs from the certainty of walking every day towards heaven, our ultimate goal, for which we were created and where we will be together, happy forever.

I wish you a joyful and serene morning!

May my blessing, which I impart with particular benevolence to the organizers, participants and all their dear ones, be propitious to you.

Christ...Strength
and Inspiration

During the general audience of November 7, 1979, Pope John Paul II addressed the president, faculty and students of the Loyola University as follows.

I am happy to receive a visit from the President of Loyola University, Chicago, and from the students and faculty of the Rome Center. You have an important part to play in deciding the future of your country and of the world. The challenges you will face will be serious ones. In Christ you will find the inspiration and the strength to meet those challenges with courage and in truth, with awareness of the true greatness of your humanity and with respect for the individual human dignity of all others. I ask Him to bless you, both now and in the future.

Bring Light
and Joy Everywhere

Because of inclement weather the general audience of November 14, 1979, was held indoors in St. Peter's Basilica and Paul VI Audience Hall. Pope John Paul II spoke the following words to the young people there.

With particular affection I address my greeting to you, young people: both because children always attract the parents' loving gaze, and because you never let the cause that you embrace with faith fall into coldness and neglect.

If, then—as is true—you believe in Christ, in the Church, and in the redemption of men through truth, you are lovers, cultivators and indefatigable propagators of this truth, which, like the sun, brings light and joy everywhere. May my blessing sustain you and accompany you.

Live in the Truth
and for the Truth!

After the Angelus on November 25, 1979, the Holy Father received in audience in the Clementine Hall the winners of the "Veritas" Competition organized by the Student Movement of Catholic Action. The competition was open to the students of the upper secondary schools of all the Italian dioceses, and the theme was taken from Paul VI's last exhortation for the World Day of Peace: "To reach peace, teach peace." His Holiness spoke to them as follows.

Beloved young people, winners of the "Veritas" Competition!

It is with particular joy that I receive you at this special meeting, expressly reserved for you, and bid you a fatherly and affectionate welcome.

You are, in fact, the winners of that interesting and significant initiative, launched by Catholic Action at the beginning of every year in all the dioceses of Italy among the students of the upper secondary schools, for the thirtieth time this year, in order to make the study of Christian faith more dynamic, enthusiastic and fruitful. I express to you, therefore, my congratulations on your diligence in studying and reflecting on the subject assigned; and at the same time I extend my grateful greeting to all the priests and teachers who enlightened and guided you methodically and lovingly.

Thank the Lord for your limpid and ardent youth, which has been, and still is, aroused to enthusiasm by sublime and salvific realities! Know that the Pope is pleased with you; but above all Jesus is pleased, Jesus the divine Friend, whom the liturgy makes us contemplate today as "King of the Universe."

You remember the touching episode in the Gospel of St. John. When the Governor Pontius Pilate asks Jesus about His real identity, He answers: "...I am a king. For this I was born, and for this I have come into the world, to bear witness to the truth. Everyone who is of the truth hears my voice." And Pilate adds thoughtfully: "What is truth?" (Jn. 18:37)

Dear young people: be bearers of the "message of Truth" in the world, be witnesses to Christ, the Way, the Truth and the Life, the Light of the world and the Salvation of mankind! By your example, show everyone that the truth must be loved! The truth must be known and, therefore, sought with love, dedication and method, and above all the truth must be lived. Christianity is not just a doctrine: it is first of all a Person, Jesus Christ, who must be loved and consequently imitated and realized in everyday life, by means of complete faith in His word, the life of grace, prayer and charity to brothers.

Beloved young people! Continue to live in the truth and for the truth! May the Blessed Virgin, the Seat of Wisdom, Mother of the Word who enlightens every man, assist you, enlighten you and comfort you.

With these wishes I impart to you my apostolic blessing, which I extend with particular benevolence to your priests and to all your dear ones.

Give Spiritual Value
to Your Actions

During the general audience of December 5, 1979, Pope John Paul II spoke the following words to the young people in St. Peter's Square.

Beloved young people, dear boys and girls,

I address to you my cordial greeting and, since we are at the beginning of the new liturgical year, I wish to exhort you to live the time of Advent intensely, and to enter "the spirit of the liturgy," which is a great help in giving spiritual value to your actions, and to enjoy the joys and consolations that come from intimacy with Christ.

May the liturgy, well known and lived, make you joyful and courageous Christians!

With this wish I impart to you my special blessing.

It Is Necessary
To Pray More

On December 16, 1979, thousands of Roman children crowded St. Peter's Square for the Angelus in order to sing to the Pope their Christmas greetings, in Italian and Polish, and to have their Christmas cribs blessed by him. In the course of his address, the Holy Father appealed for the release of a young boy, Marco Forgione, who had been kidnapped the month before. He appealed also for the release of the many other victims of kidnapping in Italy, who are still in the hands of their captors.

I now address, with special tenderness, all you boys and girls of the elementary schools of Rome, who, together with your parents and the Director of Education, have come in such large numbers to have blessed by the Pope, as last year, the images of the Baby Jesus, which you will later put in the crib prepared in your homes.

I sincerely congratulate you on this inspiring ceremony, which, with its evocative power, recalls to our mind the human and divine scene of the crib. From the time of its first representation, made, as is known, by St. Francis at Greccio on Christmas night in 1223, it has never ceased, and still continues, with its most varied traditions rich in art, poetry and folklore, to fascinate popular sentiment and Christian piety.

Here in Rome, furthermore, in addition to devotion to the Child Jesus of the Christmas cribs, there is a particular devotion to the holy Babe, throughout the whole year, in the Church of St. Mary of Aracoeli. Children pray to Him there and write Him letters, which they place at His feet.

In this time that precedes Christmas, prepare your spirit to receive the Child Jesus with faith and love, like the shepherds who walked towards the cave: "Let us go over to Bethlehem and see this thing that has happened, which the Lord has made known to us" (Lk. 2:15).

Like them, draw inspiration, you too, from the crib, to glorify and praise God, to become better and nicer, and to revive faith in Him who "lies in an earthly refuge, but reigns in heavenly splendor" (cf. St. Ambrose, *Ex. in Lucam*, II, 43).

I wish, furthermore, to call upon you to pray for vocations. In this period of expectation of the Lord, in fact, the grace of God is granted to the Church in a more generous way and more effectively reaches those who open their hearts to it. Advent is a time of specially good spiritual harvest.

Therefore, in these days, in conformity with the spirit of the Church, it is necessary to pray more, in order that the grace of vocation, both priestly and religious, may mature in the souls of the young.

Vocation is always a gift of God to a given person, but it is also a gift to the Church.

This gift is expressed in a positive response to Christ's call. This response is a particularly precious offer which we can lay beside the Christmas crib. So let us pray to the Lord to continue to call to His service, and for the called to respond generously to His invitation.

So let us now recite the Angelus for this intention, after which I will bless the statuettes of the Child Jesus that you have with you.

After the recitation of the Angelus and the prayer of blessing for the images of the Child Jesus, John Paul II then made the following appeal for little Marco Forgione.

The joy of this day, which sees so many children around the Pope preparing serenely for Christmas, is dimmed, unfortunately, by the thought that other children of their age are not able to look forward to the forthcoming feasts with the same joyful hope.

I am thinking at this moment of little Marco Forgione, kidnapped at Cosenza last month, who will be ten years old on the day before Christmas Eve. His voice, and that of other persons in the same painful situation, reaches my heart, together with that of the members of their families, fraught with anxiety and anguish. It is this deep grief of innocent souls and of families stricken in their most intimate affections that induces me to make a sorrowful appeal to the kidnappers. May the grace of Christmas touch their hearts, turning them from their resolutions, and induce them to restore the dear ones to their families, giving them all the joy of being able to embrace them, safe and sound. May this announcement, which I have given to you at the end, cause you, too, to pray for this child of your own age, and for all children in Italy and in the world in the period of preparation for Christmas and during Christmas itself.

Christmas Witnesses

On the morning of December 22, 1979, John Paul II received over fifty boys and girls of Italian Catholic Action and spoke to them as follows.

Beloved boys and girls of Catholic Action, who have come from Rome and all the regions of Italy to wish the Pope a Merry Christmas, representing also your friends.

I greet you cordially and, in you, I intend to greet all members of Italian Catholic Action for Boys and Girls; I wish, in fact, to extend my affectionate Christmas greeting to all boys and girls in the world, entrusting to you the task of announcing to all that the Pope loves them as Jesus loves them!

So thank you for your visit and your good wishes, so sincere and spontaneous, which are a moving act of faith and devotion to the Vicar of Christ.

In return for your generous courtesy, I willingly reciprocate with my fervent wishes.

And my wish is, in the first place, that you may always be aware of the real value of Christmas. What does this great and solemn event mean, which took place in the humility and silence of the stall in Bethlehem? You know: Christmas reminds us that God Himself, the Creator of the universe, wished to become a man like us, His creatures, wished to be born of Blessed Mary, in a miraculous but real way, and to accept, like us, everyday life, with all its joys and its sorrows.

Jesus is the Second Person of the Blessed Trinity, who assumed human nature in Himself: This is such a sensational and unique event that it overwhelms human history. God became like us!

Keep alive, beloved boys and girls, the real meaning of Christmas; always be aware of its true significance: Jesus was born for each of us, for every man, for every boy and girl, even if they do not know it and do not know Him; He was born to love us, to save us, to show us the real meaning of life. So always keep alive the real joy of Christmas, which is immense, interior, supernatural joy. This is the joy I wish for you now and always.

The second wish is that you may always be witnesses to Christmas during your life and in whatever place you are.

To be witnesses to Christmas means accepting the message of Jesus as definitive and decisive, because it is divine. Jesus is the Incarnate Word; He is the "Word of God" made man to communicate the truth, to reveal, to illuminate humanity about its eternal destiny. Jesus is the Light; it is not possible to do without Him!

To be witnesses to Christmas means living the presence of Jesus in us by means of "grace" and the Eucharist. The memory of the historical Christmas must become a commitment for the mystical Christmas, which is always present deep in the soul and which is mysteriously renewed in the Eucharistic meeting by means of Holy Communion. Always be friends of Jesus in the Eucharist, in order to be able to enjoy always the joy of Christmas.

To be witnesses to Christmas also means changing one's life into a gift of charity and generosity to all persons. Spiritual charity with kindness, docility, prayer and with help for all those who are suffering in poverty, illness and abandonment. But also complete charity, responding generously and totally to the priestly or religious vocation, if one feels called to this superior state of life.

Beloved boys and girls!

Spend Christmas in joy, beside your cribs, beside your parents and relatives, to whom you will take my good wishes, too.

May our Lady assist you. May my affectionate blessing accompany you.

"Sing to the Newborn Child! Proclaim Joy!"

At noon on Christmas Day, 1979, Pope John Paul II delivered his Christmas message from the balcony (loggia) of the Basilica. During the message, he spoke affectionately to the young people present there.

And now from the assembly hall of the United Nations Organization let us return to the stable at Bethlehem. Let us pause once more before the manger. And through that newborn Child let us say *to all the children of the world:* "You are our love, you are our future!" We want to pass on to you all the best things that we have. We want to pass on to you a better and more just world: *a world of human brotherhood and peace.*

We want to pass on to you the fruit of the work of all the generations and the heritage of all civilizations.

We want to pass on to you, above all, that *supreme heritage,* that never-ending Gift, that has been brought to us by the Child born in Bethlehem!

Come to Him, all of you! All the children of the whole human family! *Sing in all the languages and dialects!*

Sing to the newborn Child! Proclaim joy!

Proclaim the great joy! The joy of your feast!

And now, with a special remembrance for the children living in so many parts of the world, I wish to express a Christmas greeting in different languages....

A blessed Christmas, in the joy and peace of Christ!

Bearers of Hope

On January 2, 1980, the Holy Father spoke a special word of greeting to the young people present at the general audience.

I wish to address a special affectionate greeting today to the young boys and girls present at this audience. Beloved in Christ! You are the bearers of hope for the eighties! May the beginning of this new year be for you a spur to introduce with your life in modern society the fruitful ferments of good, love, peace, and solidarity, contained in the message of Jesus, and which are capable of truly renewing the world.

I Have Come Here Because I Love You

On January 6, 1980, the Holy Father went to the Institute of re-education at Casal del Marmo. The Pope's meeting with over sixty boys waiting to be tried took place in the chapel of the prison-school. John Paul II delivered the following address.

Beloved boys,

I am really happy to be here, among you, on this feast of the Epiphany of the Lord, in order to express to you my sincere and heartfelt wishes for the New Year, which I hope will be serene, happy and constructive.

I thank, in the first place, your Father Chaplain for the cordial words with which he wished to manifest your feelings of welcome. To you I address my greeting and good wishes with the invitation of the prophet Isaiah, which rang out in today's liturgy, and which he addressed to the holy city, Jerusalem: "Arise, shine; for your light has come, and the glory of the Lord has risen upon you" (Is. 60:1).

Dear youths, awaken and rejoice, because light has come for everyone; the glory of the Lord has been manifested; His mercy and His love shine forth above each of us to drive away and disperse any shadow that may veil and weigh upon our hearts. His radiant star has come out to illuminate all men, all of us. The Savior is "the true light that enlightens every man" (Jn. 1:9). He brought everyone "grace and truth" *(ibid.* 1:17), thus offering each one the capacity of detecting good and carrying it out, by means of the communication of divine life.

The Pope Feels Close to You

I rejoice in reflecting together with you on these certain revealed truths, because the Pope feels particularly close to all those who are, in some way, in a situation of hardship and need.

I want each of you to feel that this greeting of mine is addressed to you personally. It desires to be a moment of personal meeting, an instant of conversation and intimacy. I know your problems, I understand your difficulties; I know, in particular, how difficult it is for you to emerge from your intimate and often unconfessed anguish and look to the future with confidence; however, I would like you to become aware of the strength, unforeseeable and concealed, that lies in your youth, which is such as to be able to blossom out in an industrious future.

Sometimes we are lamps without light, with possibilities not realized, not burning. Well, I have come to light in your hearts a flame, should the disappointments you have suffered, the expectations that have not come true, have extinguished it. I want to say to each of you that you have capacities of good, honesty and industry; real, deep capacities, often unsuspected, sometimes made even greater and more vigorous by hard experience itself.

Rest assured that I have come in your midst because I love you, and have confidence in you; to manifest to you personally this affection, this trust of mine; and to tell you that I do not fail to raise my prayer to God so that He may always sustain you with that love which He manifested by sending us His only-begotten Son, Jesus Christ, our Brother. He, too, experienced suffering and need, but He indicated to us the way and offers us His help to overcome them. If you should sometimes be seized by the sad thought: people look at me with eyes that humiliate and mortify; perhaps even my dear ones do not have confidence in me— well, rest assured that the Pope addresses you with esteem, as youths who have the capacity of doing so much good in life tomorrow, and he relies on your responsible integration in society.

In this connection, I wish to express my hearty congratulations to all those who, in particular in this institute, surround you devotedly with care and attention, keeping in mind your human formation and above all the calling forth of those positive energies, those generous impulses, which must prepare in you the mature man of tomorrow, capable of doing what is good and putting himself in the service of others.

It is a necessary, delicate and difficult task, which calls for self-forgetfulness and a strong commitment. The Pope gives his fervent gratitude to all those who zealously carry out such an important task of training and discipline, admonition and guidance.

Thus, I cannot forget, together with the dedication of the personnel of the institute, at all levels, the specialized contribution of professional operators, who dedicate to your specific requirements the insight of their scientific preparation and above all the resources of their hearts.

Praise for Chaplain
and Workers

I address a thought of sincere satisfaction to the chaplain, generously made available by the Congregation of Tertiary Capuchins of Our Lady of Sorrows, and to those who, with him, have care of your souls and are concerned to offer you the gift of the Word of God, the sacraments and all those spiritual aids which facilitate your commitment of renewal and of courageous community initiatives for good.

In this perspective, I consider worthy of mention and praise the group of voluntary workers who cooperate even within your dwelling, to set up family relations with you and create around you a larger community of friends, concerned with your spiritual and material good.

Those who are responsible for your education are certainly aware that you, too—like all those of your age—constitute the hope of the years to come. They cannot forget that there exist in your hearts—experience teaches us—an emotional impetus, often exasperated by bitter solitude, an affective vitality, rich in acute intuitions, an imaginative originality, which, unable to find a legitimate expression, often owing to adverse circumstances, may have led you along bad and dangerous paths. It is necessary, therefore, to give you and all those in your situation —studied with penetrating perspicacity and reliable competence—a real possibility of reintegration and renewal, so that you will be able, with the assistance of all good members of society, to turn to good use and service the impetuous strength in your hearts.

Need of Your Responsible Cooperation

Dear boys, this reflection, concerning rather the role of those who undertake generously and rightfully the task of your physical, intellectual, moral and spiritual education, turns me again to you, in concluding this affectionate talk of mine.

You put forward justified rights with regard to society; you are waiting for help; you are aware that laws and courts are not sufficient to form new men, capable of acting in an upright way, but that a civil structure is necessary which will operate in the direction of brotherhood, in respect of ethical and moral values, in enlightened exemplarity, in obedience to the law of God, the Sovereign Good, on account of which it is necessary to avoid evil—that is, all that offends, in the most concrete situations, God Himself and our neighbor. A society in which there is not a strong moral inspiration, which is not illuminated by a superior light, which does not hold in due respect all the expressions of human life and its dignity, will not be able to offer valuable contributions for renewal, active participation, and a firm hand to all those who have often been victims of selfishness or of deficiencies for which they are not responsible.

From the Church, too, from the community of those who wish to bear witness to Christ, you expect consistency of faith and works, which will qualify it to instill vital certainties and human behavior, worthy of Him who gave Himself completely to brothers unto the last sacrifice. You rightly ask for a spiritual and material solidarity which will enable you to integrate yourselves successfully in civil society.

However—and here let each of you withdraw into himself for mature reflection—your future, secure and prosperous as you wish it to be, cannot be constructed without you, without your responsible cooperation. You are, in fact, the real architects and the ones mainly responsible—on the human plane—for your future.

Life, a Gift from God

May the light of the star of Bethlehem, which is the light of Jesus, make you understand the depth of the commitment that is required of you; may it enlighten you about your duties. Life is a real gift from God, which is always worth accepting gratefully and courageously, in awareness that, from an existence lived with honesty, faithfulness and hope, you will be able to draw concrete fruits of personal satisfaction and ensure valuable advantages for society.

This task may seem superior to your strength, but you are not alone in tackling it, since the Lord, our Father and Friend, has your personal destiny at heart in a far more effective and loving way than you can, perhaps, imagine. Present in us by means of the grace received at Baptism, He loves us faithfully even when we fall into sin and He never leaves us alone, in any circumstance. Therefore, turn with extreme confidence in prayer to Him who is beside you, in you, and entrust yourselves with special devotion to the Blessed Virgin who, with tenderness and motherly solicitude, wishes to accompany you and sustain you at every step of your way.

Your "Father Agostino"

May you be encouraged and strengthened by the affectionate blessing which I now impart to you, together with the dearly loved Cardinal, my Secretary of State, and always your dear "Father Agostino," who has been following you and loving you for so many years, and instilling in you, faithfully, the resources of his priestly spirit. Together we wish you a year rich in heavenly favors, and together we invoke on you the blessing of the Lord, which we implore also on your families, that God may assist them and help them in all their necessities and give them, in you, the consolations that they are entitled to expect from you; as well as on all those who dedicate their attention and their care to you, beginning with the superiors and assistants who spend such a large part of their lives beside you.

The Star Is Jesus!

During the general audience of January 9, 1980, Pope John Paul II addressed the young people on the significance of imitating Jesus.

And now I address you, beloved young people, boys and girls present at this audience, to extend to you my special greeting and good wishes.

We are still near the great feasts of Christmas and Epiphany, and so I renew my exhortation to keep your eyes fixed on the luminous star at Bethlehem, as the Wise Men from the East did.

The Star is Jesus, because He alone, in the tumult and travail of history and of our own existence, indicates to us the right way for our life and helps us to walk along it. It is my heartfelt wish for you that the New Year, just started, will be for you all a year of deep friendship with Jesus, deepening your knowledge of the Gospel, living in His grace, imitating Him in charity toward your neighbor.

And may my fatherly blessing also accompany you!

Conversion, Communion, Mission

In the afternoon of January 13, 1980, the Holy Father visited the Pontifical Irish College where he celebrated Mass. After the Gospel, Pope John Paul gave the following homily.

Moladh go deo le Dia.
Praised be Jesus Christ.
Dearly beloved in Christ,

Today, once again, in a very special way, the Pope belongs to Ireland.

After my visit to your land, it is a joy for me to come to the Pontifical Irish College and meet all those who live here: the priests and seminarians, and the Sisters of Saint John of God. My visit is also meant for the community of St. Isidore's Franciscan College and St. Patrick's Augustinian College. With the Cardinal Primate of All Ireland and with brothers in the Episcopate, including former rectors of the Irish College, we are celebrating together our unity in Jesus Christ and in His Church.

The place of our celebration is important for its contribution to the Church, for the impact it has had on the lives of the Irish, and for its responsibility to future generations. It is likewise important for the Christian witness of love that has been given here; one example well known to me is the hospitality furnished by the Irish College to Polish refugees after the Second World War. In this regard, the presence at this Mass of Monsignor Denis MacDaid is a living link with the splendid achievements of the past.

And so, with our history and our hopes, all of us are here together to seek light and strength in commemorating the Baptism of the Lord. As portrayed in the Gospels, the Baptism of Jesus marked the beginning of His public ministry. John the Baptist proclaimed the need for conversion, and the great mystery of divine communion was revealed: the Holy Spirit descended on Christ, and God the Father pointed out His beloved Son to the world. From that moment on, Jesus pursued resolutely His mission of salvation. Our celebration today invites us to reflect personally on these three elements: conversion, communion and mission.

The role of John was to prepare for Christ. It was in the context of conversion that the communion existing in the life of the most Holy Trinity was revealed. The Baptist was announcing an invitation to turn to God, to be conscious of sin, to repent, to walk in the truth of one's relationship with God. Meanwhile, Jesus Himself had submitted to the penitential rite and was at prayer when the voice of the Father proclaimed Him as Son: the One who is *totus ad Patrem,* the One who is totally devoted to the Father and living for Him, the One totally enveloped in His love. We too are called to take on the attitude of Jesus towards His Father. The condition, however, for this is conversion: a daily, repeated, constant, sustained turning to God. Conversion is necessary to express the truth of the adoption of sons that is ours in Baptism. For in Baptism we were called to union with Christ in His death and resurrection, and hence we were called to die to sin and to live for God. In

Baptism the vivifying action of the Holy Spirit took place in us, and the Father now sees in us His only Son, Jesus Christ: "You are my Son, the Beloved; my favor rests on you" (Lk. 3:22).

The communion of the most Holy Trinity goes on in our lives. Through Jesus Christ, the mystery of divine adoption takes place (cf. Eph. 1:5; Gal. 4:5), as He who is the *Unigenitus Dei Filius* becomes the *Primogenitus in multis fratribus* (Rom. 8:29). A former student of the Irish college, the Servant of God, Dom Columba Marmion, has left to you and to the whole Church extensive writings of deep insight and great value on this mystery of the divine Sonship and on the centrality of Jesus Christ in God's plan of sanctification.

In our daily lives the call to conversion and divine communion has practical requirements, if we are to walk in the profound truth of our vocation, in the sincerity of our relationship with the Father, through Christ and in the Holy Spirit. In practice, there must be an openness to the Father and to each other. Remember that Jesus is *totus ad Patrem,* and that He wanted the world to listen to Him say: "I love the Father" (Jn. 14:31). Just this last week in my Wednesday audience I mentioned that man fulfills his nature only by "existing 'with someone'—and still more profoundly and more completely: existing 'for someone' " (Discourse of January 9, 1980). These words in turn reflect the teaching of the Second Vatican Council on the social nature of man (cf. *Gaudium et spes,* nos. 12, 25).

We who in our ministry are called to form community on the supernatural basis of divine communion must first experience community ourselves in faith and love. This experience of community is one that is rooted in the earliest traditions of the Church: we too must be of one heart and one soul, united in the teaching of the Apostles, in fellowship, in the breaking of bread and in prayers (cf. Acts 4:32; 2:42).

To walk in the truth of our vocation means striving to please God rather than men, to be just in God's sight. It means a lifestyle that corresponds to the reality of our role in the Church today, a lifestyle that takes into account the needs of our brethren and the ministry that we shall exercise tomorrow. Living the truth in love is a challenge to the simplicity of our lives, and to a self-discipline that manifests itself in diligent work and study—in responsible and accountable preparation for our mission of service to God's people.

In a special way, living the truth of our lives here and now—in Rome in the year 1980—means fidelity to prayer, to contact with Jesus, to communion with the Blessed Trinity. The evangelist points out that it was while Jesus was in prayer that the mystery of the Father's love was manifested and the communion of the Three Divine Persons was revealed. It is in prayer that we learn the mystery of Christ and the wisdom of the cross. In prayer we perceive, in all their dimensions, the real needs of our brothers and sisters throughout the world; in prayer we are strengthened for the choices that lie ahead; in prayer we are fortified for the mission that Christ shares with us: to bring "true justice to the nations...to serve the cause of right" (Is. 42:1, 6).

Hence, this house and all the religious houses and seminaries of Rome are meant to be houses of prayer, where Christ is formed in every generation. Because you are living in Rome, in a diocese for which I personally must give a particular accounting to the Lord, you will understand how ardently I desire that Christ should be formed in you (cf. Gal. 4:19).

But towards this goal you must not walk alone. In a community of brethren who maintain alive and pure the same high ideals of Christ's priesthood you will find strength and support. In the communion of the Church you will find joy. Through the guidance of competent spiritual directors you will find encouragement and you will avoid self-deception; by turning to them you will, above all, render homage to the humanity of the Incarnate Word of God, who continues to sustain and guide the Church through the instrumentality of men.

And as you endeavor to accept fully the call to conversion and communion—the call to full life in Christ—the sense of your mission must grow more and more acute. In tranquility and trust you must begin to experience ever more a sense of urgency: the urgency to communicate Christ and His saving Gospel.

By the grace of God there is now going on in Ireland a period of intense spiritual renewal, and all of you must become involved in this. You must prepare yourselves for this mission by work and study and, especially, prayer. In this regard I ask you to listen once again to the words I prepared for the students at Maynooth: "What I really want you to realize is this: that God counts on you, that He makes His plans, in a way, depend on your free collaboration, on the oblation of your lives, and on the generosity with which you follow the inspirations of the Holy Spirit in the depths of your hearts. The Catholic Faith of Ireland today was linked, in God's plan, to the fidelity of St. Patrick. And tomorrow, yes, tomorrow some part of God's plan will be linked to your fidelity—to the fervor with which you say *yes* to God's word in your lives."

The youth of Ireland have understood and responded very well to my call, the call to come to Christ who is "the way and the truth and the life." But they need your special gift, your help, your ministry, your priesthood, so that they can succeed in living the truth of their Christian vocation. Do not let them down. Go among them and be recognized, like the Apostles, as men who have been with Jesus (cf. Acts 4:13), men who have been steeped in His word, and are aflame with His zeal: "I must preach the good news of the kingdom of God...for I was sent for this purpose" (Lk. 4:43). But the success of this mission of yours depends on the authenticity of your conversion, on the degree that you are conformed to Jesus Christ, the beloved Son of the eternal Father, the Son of Mary. Turn to her and ask her help.

In the Eucharist that I am celebrating with you and for you today, I have present in my heart your families and friends, and the entire Irish nation. In a special way I am praying for the youth of Ireland. And today, to you and through you to all of them, I wish to say once again: "Young people of Ireland, I love you! Young people of Ireland, I bless you! I bless you in the name of our Lord Jesus Christ." Amen.

Truth,
the Power of Peace

After the Angelus, the Pope addressed over four thousand children and young people of Catholic Action of the diocese of Rome, taking part in the "Caravan of peace."

I now address my cordial greeting to the numerous groups of boys and girls and children of Catholic Action of the diocese of Rome, who, among the various spiritual, cultural and sports events to which they dedicate themselves in their respective parishes, have wished to organize jointly the "Caravan of peace." They show in this way that they have welcomed enthusiastically the indication: "truth, the power of peace," which I proposed in the message for the "World Day of Peace"; and they acknowledge publicly that they have understood the necessity of brotherly solidarity with the underprivileged in life.

Thanking you for your presence, beloved children, I wish to encourage you to let God, the Truth and infinite Love, always inspire your thoughts and actions, in order to contribute to the construction of a more just and serene society. In human society, in which, unfortunately, there are so many conflicts today, overcome the temptations of selfishness and indifference, to bear witness to Christ's charity everywhere.

I invoke divine assistance on your generous resolutions, and I willingly bless you, extending the apostolic blessing to all your dear ones.

Complete Answers in Christ

After the Angelus message on January 27, 1980, the Holy Father addressed a greeting to a special group of young people.

I now greet cordially the young men and women belonging to the movement "Communion and Liberation," who have come in large numbers to Rome from Central and Southern Italy for a spiritual retreat, and who are present here to testify their affection for the Pope.

Beloved sons, you know how much I appreciate your generous commitment and how much I trust in youth.

Today I wish to exhort you once more to live your Christianity completely and consistently. In Christ you will discover the real greatness of your dignity as human beings, created in the image and likeness of God (Gn. 1:26). In Him you will always find the answer to your problems and your questions in the various circumstances of life and expectations of society. May He always be your light, your comfort and your strength to bear witness with your life to the true values that Christ brought to the world.

May my blessing accompany you.

Do Not Be Afraid

Pope John Paul II spoke briefly to the students of Rome's Notre Dame International School during the public audience of January 30, 1980.

My cordial greetings go also to the students and faculty of the Notre Dame International School of Rome. It is a real joy for me to see so many of you here today. What I want to tell you is what I told the young people in America: "Do not be afraid of honest effort and honest work; do not be afraid of the truth.... Open your hearts to the Christ of the Gospels —to His love and His truth and His joy." God bless you all.

When Youth Are Won for Christ...

During the same audience the Holy Father expressed his joy and hope in the young people of "GEN."

I greet cordially the young people present here: Among them there is the GEN group of the Focolari who, coming from all over the world, are gathered these days at the Mariapolis Center at Rocca di Papa for their annual Congress. The young, as you know, are for me a growing source of joy and hope, because, when they are won over by Christ, they give everything, like the boy in the Gospel (cf. Jn. 6:9), who offers his loaves and his fish, which give rise to the miracle.

To you my blessing; may it accompany you throughout your lives.

Loyalty and Fair Play

On February 9, 1980, the Holy Father received managers and athletes of the Ascoli football team, who had come to the Vatican together with the members of their families from Ascoli Piceno. The group was led by Bishop Marcello Morgante of Ascoli.
John Paul II delivered the following address.

Dear managers and players of Ascoli-Calcio!

I willingly agreed to your desire to be received by me in audience, because I know the kind sentiments you have for my person, and also—as your Bishop confirms to me— the sincerity of your faith as Christians. But I agreed all the more readily because in this way I have the privilege of paying a debt of my venerated Predecessor, Paul VI, who, some years ago, at the beginning of your rise in the greatest national championship, received a similar request, to which, however, he was unable to give a positive answer owing to other urgent commitments of ministry.

That is why today's meeting takes on a particular and, I would say, more definite and rich character. The word I address to you aims at being a simple and sincere one, which goes to your persons, to the sporting profession, and is extended by analogy and I would say, rather, association of ideas to religious and moral life.

I wish to express, in the first place, my congratulations to you individuals and at the same time to the Association to which you belong, which right from its foundation in distant 1898 has won well-deserved successes. Ascoli-Calcio has been active since that date, and gradually, through the unanimous effort of technicians and athletes, but also owing to the fervor of the citizens who shared enthusiastically in this effort, it has arrived at the honor of belonging to the football teams of the 1st division and —what is more important—of pitting itself against them in a great many matches. It is no mean achievement, if we think that the city, though noble and ancient, is relatively small in area and number of inhabitants. My hearty congratulations!

But this success of yours, the victories that constitute it and also the efforts and sacrifices it involves, prompt me to pass from the value and significance of sport to the value and significance of human life, of which the former is—as history confirms—an important and constant manifestation. In this connection, some highly significant words of the Apostle St. Paul come to my aid: in the first of his two letters to the faithful of the city of Corinth, which was, in ancient Greece, the famous seat of the Isthmian Games, he wished to draw a suitable teaching of religious character from the practice of sport. To exhort those children of his of whom he had become "the father in Christ Jesus through the gospel" and urge them to imitate himself (cf. 1 Cor. 4:15-16), he conjured up the image, a usual one for them, of the runners and wrestlers in the stadium, who, to obtain the prize reserved for only one of them, submitted to all kinds of sacrifices: "They do it"—the Apostle commented—"to receive a perishable wreath, but we an imperishable" (*ibid.* 9:24-25).

This is the lesson, beloved sons and brothers, that I wish to propose to you in memory of this familiar and welcome meeting: to the wish that your sporting profession may always be inspired by the noble ideals of loyalty and courage, fair play and chivalry, I add the wish for your Christian profession which, far from being extraneous to, or in contradiction with, the former, must obviously rather integrate it, with the contribution also of other factors, and at the same time elevate it in order that your personality itself may be complete. Christianity is in itself a religion that calls for an earnest and strong commitment in the spiritual and moral field, and today especially—in the eyes of a world that is so often heedless or indifferent—it becomes credible only if expressed, in the lives of individual Christians, in a consistent and transparent profession of life. And profession—mark you—means almost the same as confession—that is, it is a kind of declaring and bearing witness with actions to what one is. In simpler words I want to say to you: As you are good football players, endeavor also to be good Christians, always faithful to the Lord, to His Church and to His law of love for Himself and the brethren.

May the propitiating apostolic blessing, which I now willingly impart to you and extend to your relatives and friends, strengthen you in this commitment.

Have Confidence, Victory Is Ours!

In the Hall of Benedictions, February 13, 1980, Pope John Paul II addressed a large group of children and youth.

Dear young people, boys and girls,

The applause and the joyful welcome you gave me as I was entering this Hall, passing through your groups, differing in age and in the school classes to which you belong, but unanimous in enthusiasm, already reveal in themselves your sincere hearts, the interest you take in the events of faith, and the affection you cherish for the Church and for the Pope, her visible Head.

I greet you all cordially and thank you for the joy you give me with your significant presence. In the first place, you who have come here together with your parents, your teachers and your parish priests at the end of the catechetical courses which prepared you to receive devoutly and fruitfully the sacraments of First Communion and Confirmation; and then I greet all the others coming from elementary and secondary schools, among which I am happy to mention two Roman Institutes: the Modern Language High School of the Sacred Heart at Trinità dei Monti, and the "Virgil" High School.

My thought goes in the first place to your educators for the constant care they dedicate to you boys in the various environments of family, academic and recreational life; for the work they carry out, with wisdom and love, to make you grow, like the boy Jesus, "in wisdom and in stature, and in favor with God and man" (Lk. 2:52).

You are certainly aware of the importance that Jesus Himself gave to children, who often became the protagonists of some pages of the Gospel and were even held up as models for adults: "Unless you turn and become like children, you will never enter the kingdom of heaven" (Mt. 18:3; Mk. 10:15; Lk. 18:17; Jn. 3:3). They are the object of such a tender welcome that it might seem inconceivable, in view of the mysterious elevation of His personality, if the facts were not there to reassure us. Was it not He who said to His disciples: "Let the children come to me"? (Mk. 10:14; Mt. 19:14; Lk. 18:16)

Before such predilection, not only the little children of the elementary schools, but also the ones who are bigger and who attend secondary schools, must draw a stimulus to love Jesus more and more, meet Him, know Him and follow Him without ever tiring or withdrawing. Choose Christ as supreme Teacher and Savior. He will free you of selfish passions, arbitrary fashions and mass conformism. How many young people think they are free because they have shaken off the authority of their parents and educators, without realizing that they have become slaves of the will of a group!

Have confidence in Christ and in the Church that introduces Him to you. Have the courage to show by deed the liberating power of His charity and His teaching. In this way you will contribute to making the world better, more just and brotherly, at a moment when the violence of hatred is staining the streets of our cities with blood. All that will be a great experience for you, which will demand of you sacrifice and perhaps even heroism, but victory will be ours, because the Lord repeats to you as He once did to the fishermen of Galilee: "Take heart, it is I; have no fear" (Mk. 6:50).

With these thoughts and with these wishes I willingly invoke on you and your friends the continual protection of the Lord and the fullness of His blessings.

Like Mary,
Rejoice in Your Vocation

After his visit to the Lateran University, on February 16, 1980, the Pope went to the Major Seminary where he prayed Vespers with the seminarians and numerous young persons of Rome who are accustomed to pray in the seminary. The Holy Father spoke to the group as follows.

Dear seminarians,

On this day, dedicated to the Feast of Our Lady of Confidence, there could not fail to take place, after the visit to the Pontifical Lateran University, a meeting with you, whom I feel more particularly close to my heart, and who represent the hope of this Church of Rome.

Here, we are in the very heart of the diocese: beside the episcopal cathedral, where flourishes and works a well-deserving institute of sacred sciences, which proposes to present and study more deeply the living Magisterium of the Roman Pontiff and of the whole Catholic Episcopate; and, still within a few steps of the Lateran Basilica, there also rises the building that houses the future priests, the future collaborators of the Bishop. For this reason, the seminary is the most delicate and sensitive part of this heart. Its walls, in fact, give hospitality to youths who, wishing to give their lives a generous and committed expression, propose to follow the Lord Jesus more closely along the paths of the world, to be stewards of the divine mysteries (cf. 1 Cor. 4:1).

I am happy, therefore, to be in your midst, to pour out with you to the Lord, more than words, the fresh liveliness of feelings and thoughts addressed to the necessities of this beloved Roman diocese and of the other dioceses to which you belong.

Together with the Cardinal Vicar, who helps me to bear the pastoral responsibilities of the ecclesial community, I address in the first place to the rector, to his collaborators and to you all, a grateful greeting for the fervent invitation; a greeting full of hope for your future, and also accompanied by the exhortation to listen faithfully and joyfully to Him who has called you in an effective and irresistible tone: "Come, follow me" (cf. Mt. 19:21).

I also address a special thought to you young people, who often gather here to take part in meetings of prayer and reflection, which can illuminate the lofty ideal of giving oneself entirely to love of Christ (cf. Rom. 10:15) in priestly life.

The Joy of the Soul in God

Let us now dwell on the passage of Isaiah which was proposed to us in the celebration of these solemn Vespers, to draw some useful considerations from it.

At the beginning of the chapter, the prophet, with words that recall a priestly investiture, announces that he has received a message of consolation with regard to Israel (cf. Is. 61:1ff.). With Israel, now become a people of priests, God will conclude an eternal covenant (cf. *ibid.*, 6-8), thus sketching the reality of the Church, a people redeemed. Before this messianic prospect, there bursts from the heart of the prophet a song of grateful joy: "I will greatly rejoice in the Lord; my soul shall exult in my God" (Is. 61:10).

The joy of the soul in God, manifested by Isaiah in these words, at once turns our thoughts to Mary, who expressed her joy particularly in the song of the Magnificat. Mary's joy was the joy of grace, of the gift received—that is, the vocation to be called by God to a mission which certainly represents the peak of woman's dignity and aspiration. Thanks to her, there was to be realized the great, unfathomable mystery, which the people of Israel, interpreting the desire and the expectation of the whole of mankind, kept in its most deep and living religious tradition: the presence of "Emmanuel," that is, of God with us.

Mary's joy was, therefore, joy for the trust that God had shown in her by entrusting Himself to her in the Person of His only Son. Bearing in her womb the Word Incarnate, and giving Him to the world, she became the extraordinary depositary of God's trust in man, so that Mary is rightly honored as the Mother of Divine Confidence.

The joy expressed and sung by Mary in the Magnificat was the greatest that ever penetrated and transformed the human heart; a joy united with the deepest gratitude and the most profound humility. Humility prepares and makes possible God's gift; gratitude treasures it, interiorizes it and makes space for it.

The gift offered by God is always that of the salvation of man, made just and participating in God's holiness, through a re-established relationship of loving communion, adopted filiation, and participation in divine nature. Isaiah, in fact, affirms with an expressive image: "My soul shall exult in my God, for he has clothed me with the garments of salvation, he has covered me with the robe of righteousness" (Is. 61:10); in the Magnificat, Mary sings the joy of her divine motherhood, which is salvation for everyone: "My spirit rejoices in God my Savior.... His mercy is on those who fear him from generation to generation" (Lk. 1:47-50).

To all of you gathered here, I desire to wish the same joy announced by Isaiah and lived intensely by Mary: the joy of God's salvific gift which passes through your personal vocation, the unrepeatable expression of His fatherly confidence in you. To you who are already aware and certain of your call, and of the consequent responsible commitment, I wish the joy of happy possession of the divine gift and sweet experience of it; while to those, already in the seminary or still outside it, who are in trusting quest of their own way, I wish the happiness of listening serenely to God's voice and of an explorative path, carried out in the certainty that the Lord fills the hungry with good things and helps His servants, because of His mercy (cf. Lk. 1:53-54).

To let ourselves be possessed by this joy of the Lord's, of which St. Paul wrote in the letters to the Romans (15:13) and to the Philippians (4:4), it is necessary to be faithful and respectful of the grace that God communicates to us, becoming more and more deeply aware of the gift received and more and more conscious, at the same time, of our unworthiness: "I am a man of unclean lips" (Is. 6:5). "Depart from me, for I am a sinful man, O Lord" (Lk. 5:8).

With regard to the priesthood, both we who have received it and also you who are on your way to it, can we not think, in conformity with the example of Mary, that God has granted us His trust in a very special way, and that Christ entrusts Himself also to us? Precisely through the priesthood, He has covered us with a very special robe of salvation.

Dear seminarians and dear youths, to respond to such divine trust—that is, to the grace of vocation—it is necessary above all to have confidence. The grace of the Lord is greater than our weakness; it is greater than our unworthiness, precisely as St. John expresses: "By this we shall... reassure our hearts before him whenever our hearts condemn us; for God is greater than our hearts" (1 Jn. 3:19-20). We must have invincible confidence, so as always to deserve the trust of the Lord; and Mary, who is mother of God's trust in us, will thus become, at the same time, mother of our trust in Him.

The pious invocation *"Mater mea, fiducia mea,"* so dear to all those who have been formed in this seminary, contains the deepest and fullest sense of our relationship with Mary, who is praised and venerated precisely by means of such regard of confidence, esteem and hope. In fact, "the Father's eternal love, which has been manifested in the history of mankind through the Son...comes close to each of us through this mother and thus takes on tokens that are more easily understood and accessible to each person. Consequently, Mary must be on all the ways for the Church's daily life" *(RH 22).*

Mother of Every Priest

Concluding our reflections in this way, I am happy to enclose this last exhortation of mine in an expression dear to the Marian tradition of your seminary: *"Aucti fiducia tui fac ut spem Ecclesiae cumulemus."* Sustained and strengthened by your trust in us and by our confidence in you, bring it about, O Mary, that we meet the hope of the Church. Yes, dear young men, the ways of the Church are those of Mary, and may an ever deeper confidence in her, the Mother of every priest, help you to traverse with great fruit the path of your vocation, to the real consolation of the whole Church.

With these wishes and with great affection I impart to you my special apostolic blessing.

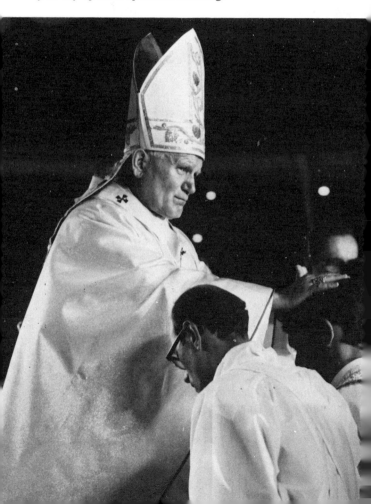

The Charity
of Good Example

In the Hall of Benedictions on Ash Wednesday (February 20, 1980), the Pope spoke to the young people on the subject of penance and conversion.

My meeting, always particularly desired with you, beloved children and young people, takes place on a day of great meditation, with a precise reminder of the necessity of being converted, of improving and ascending to the heights.

With the austere rite of the imposition of the ashes on our heads as mortal men, the Church, today, utters words that arouse deep echoes in our hearts. Her majestic and warning voice is the voice of God Himself: "Man, you are dust and to dust you shall return." Those ashes are, in fact, the symbol of the relative value of all earthly things, of the extreme precariousness and fragility of this life because of its limits, its conditionings, its contradictions and difficulties. Hence, the motherly exhortation of the Church to free the spirit from any form of disorderly attachment to earthly realities in order to be able to look confidently to the resurrection.

You, beloved children and young people, know very well, however, that the meeting with the risen Christ must be prepared for by means of a commitment of personal growth in the course of this existence of ours in time, and furthermore by means of dedication to a constructive work of human improvement and Christian animation of our surroundings. This courageous and "committed" view of life, which is so much in keeping with your generous daring, includes therefore the concepts of repentance, mortification and renunciation, which spring from a strong desire for justice and from intense love of God.

Repentance is synonymous with conversion, and conversion means overcoming everything that is contrary to the dignity of sons of God, especially the wild passions that the apostle and evangelist, St. John, calls "the lust of the flesh and the lust of the eyes and the pride of life" (1 Jn. 2:16), forces of evil that are always insidious and always conspiring though in forms that are sometimes enticing. Permanent struggle is necessary against them. The period of Lent, which begins today and which has as its purpose a sincere return to the heavenly Father, infinitely good and merciful, calls us particularly to do so.

This return, the fruit of an act of love, will be all the more expressive and agreeable to Him the more it is accompanied by the sacrifice of something necessary and, above all, of superfluous things. A vast range of actions presents itself to your free initiative, from assiduous and generous practice of your everyday duty, to humble and joyful acceptance of the troublesome incidents that may arise in the course of the day, to renunciation of something very pleasant in order to be able to help those who are in need; but above all, the charity of good example is pleasing to the Lord. It is made necessary by the fact that we belong to a family of faith, the members of which are interdependent; and each one needs help and support from all the others. Good example acts not only externally, but penetrates in depth and constructs on the other the most precious and most active good, which is that of adherence to one's own Christian vocation.

All these things are difficult to carry out; for our weak forces a supplement of energy is necessary. Where can we find it? Let us recall the words of the divine Savior: "Apart from me you can do nothing!" (Jn. 15:5) We must have recourse to Him: You know that Christ is found in the personal dialogue of prayer and, especially, in the reality of the sacraments. Lent is the most propitious time to have access to these divine sources of supernatural life. In the sacrament of Penance we become reconciled with God and with brothers; with the Eucharist we receive Christ, who sustains our weak and wavering wills.

Encouraging you to this commitment of purification and renewal, I invoke on your resolutions the assistance of the divine Spirit, and I willingly impart the apostolic blessing to you and your respective families.

Let Life Be a Song of Joy

On the morning of March 1, 1980, the Holy Father received about eight thousand students from various institutes in Rome and Latium. Among those present there was little Alfredo Battaglia, a 13-year-old boy kidnapped on October 30, 1979, and released on February 23, 1980. Pope John Paul II had made an appeal for his release in the course of the general audience on November 14th.

The Holy Father delivered the following address.

Beloved students,

It is a real joy for me today to be with you, who bring me the enthusiasm and devotion of the students of the schools of Rome. In you, belonging to elementary and junior and senior secondary schools, I see present also the other children, boys and girls and adolescents, who attend all the educational establishments of this city and of Latium. Today you are, as it were, the representatives of this vast world, and I, therefore, greet you with special cordiality. My affectionate greeting goes to each of you and to each of your schools, the list of which has just been read. In particular, I wish to mention the most numerous one, that of the Sacred Heart of Marymount, which is celebrating the fiftieth anniversary of its foundation this year.

I am also happy to express my welcome to Alfredo Battaglia, the boy who has suffered owing to the recent kidnapping. Assuring him that I was close to him with apprehension, as to all victims of kidnapping, I am glad that he is now here among us.

I heartily thank everyone for having wished to offer me this marvelous demonstration of affection and reverence.

But I also wish to address to you some words, all for yourselves, concerning your condition as young students and Christians.

Study with Industry

Your age is the most propitious season of life to sow and get ready the ground for future harvests. It is a time of preparation, so that the more serious is your commitment in carrying out your duties today, the more certain and fruitful will be the exercise of the missions entrusted to you tomorrow. And today you can exercise seriousness in your duty at various levels.

In the first place at school. Apply yourselves, therefore, to study with great industry; it stimulates, in fact, your personal maturation. Assiduous contact with the subjects of your scholastic programs cannot but be constructive, not only because it trains you in the discipline of intelligence and will, but also because it opens up to you ever new horizons on the vastness of human knowledge in its multiple historical, linguistic, mathematical, philosophical, technical, artistic manifestations, etc. Remember that, even among adults, the man who is always prepared to learn is great, while he who thinks he already knows everything is, actually, only full of himself and, therefore, empty of the great values that really enrich life. Study, therefore, with the desire of always getting to know new things, but also with much humility, because only the latter can keep you open and available for ever further acquisitions. Only he who knows that he has not yet succeeded in winning what he longs for and who, therefore, uses all his strength to attain his purpose, really arrives at new goals.

Play the Game Fairly

Secondly, I know that you devote a great deal of time to play. Well, it is necessary to know that play is not just a matter of amusement and lightheartedness; but, even when you do not realize it, it is an important opportunity of formation and virtue. Also in your future life, in fact, you will have to collaborate with and pit yourselves against other persons, before problems, situations and projects which, precisely, make life so similar to a game to be played fairly. To that will contribute the wise use of your own energies, clear knowledge of the general context in which you have taken your place, the capacity of adapting yourselves to the rhythm of others, and a loyal and generous sense of competition. That is why there can be no break between school and play: both contribute to building your personality, because both have a great deal to teach, and together they are the expression of a youth that is not only exterior but also interior.

Love Your Family

But there is also a third thing, which has great value at your age: attachment to your family, especially your parents. I hope that you all find in your homes an atmosphere of real love. But I also wish to invite you to establish, and always maintain, a relationship of great and true affection with your parents; they are your first friends. To a large extent, your life in the future depends on how you are today in harmony with, and cherish respect for, those who begot you and brought you up.

Certainly, the moment of detachment may come, and for this, too, you must train for personally responsible growth; but never cut your human and family roots, on pain of becoming arid or wild.

As you see, all that I have said so far concerns your human education, which is a very important thing.

In Harmony with All

But there is another decisive element of your life, and it is the specifically Christian one, which is grafted onto your humanity and causes it to blossom. A real Christian, that is, a holy person, is also always a perfectly harmonious man. I could mention to you so many names, but they all derive their greatness from one name only, which is that of Jesus of Nazareth, Son of God from all eternity, who became our Lord by means of His death and resurrection. His life, as you well know, was spent entirely on behalf of others. Well, you must look to Him, have Him present in your thoughts and your affections, follow Him every day, since only by Him can each of us say with full truth together with St. Paul: He "loved me and gave himself for me" (Gal. 2:20).

This is where you will draw your deepest joy, such as to become also your strength and, therefore, your support. If you, unluckily, were to meet with bitterness, undergo suffering, experience incomprehension, and even fall into sin, let your thought of faith go at once to Him who always loves you and who, precisely, with His infinite love like that of God the Father, makes us overcome every test, fills all our voids, wipes out every sin, and urges us with enthusiasm towards a way that is again safe and joyful.

Life does not spare any man on this earth such experiences. Your little troubles of today may be only a signal of greater future difficulties. But the presence of Jesus with us, "always, to the close of the age" (Mt. 28:20), is the most exalting and, at the same time, most realistic guarantee that we are not alone, but that Someone is walking with us, as that day with the two disconsolate disciples of Emmaus (cf. Lk. 24:13ff.).

Sense of the Gospel

Keep alive in you and always preserve this youthful sense of the Gospel, which the men of today need so much, and bear witness to it in your environment. I would like to tell you that it is in order not to grow old that we must cling tenaciously to Jesus and His proclamation. Only love, in fact, which is the soul of the Gospel, enables us to be always young. You know the episodes of violence of our days: how many deaths they cause, and how many tears! Well, he who causes deaths is not only old, but is already dead inside. Life, in fact, springs only from love and, therefore, from another life, or from a death faced lovingly, like that of Jesus. So cultivate the most genuine love for everyone, always ready to help those in need, to forgive those who offend you, and even to correct or at least have compassion on those who act tyrannically.

Let these, dear students, be the essential commitments of your lives. And since, as you know, we are now living in the period of Lent, try to put them into practice right away as preparation for next Easter. Your happiness will be all the more pure, the more it has passed through trial, sacrifice and self-mastery.

Your Life a Song

My wish for you, therefore, is that all your life may be so: that is, a song of joy, arising from consciousness that Jesus died for our sake, and for the beauty of our unshakable communion with Him, which we experience even in the most difficult moments.

Always rest assured that the Pope loves you! Therefore, I greet you all once more, together with your teachers and parents. May the Lord always accompany you with His grace, which I invoke on you abundantly, while I willingly grant my special apostolic blessing to everyone.

"You Are Not Alone"

Pope John Paul II spoke to the young on March 5, 1980, in St. Peter's Basilica.

It is a pleasure for me, dear boys and girls, to receive you, so joyful and affectionate, today. And you are so numerous that, today too, a special audience was necessary for you within this large Basilica, which—as you know—is built over the tomb of St. Peter, the Prince of the Apostles, the first of the Popes.

From the list of the various groups, which has just been read, I was able to note that you come from various parts of Italy, also distant ones, and that you are divided into two main categories: you belong either to school groups, or to parish groups. None of you has come alone, individually, but each one has joined persons of his own age and fellow students, the teachers of his own school or the priests of his own parish. What does this mean? I wish to put this question to myself and to you, to concentrate our reflection on the importance that the school and the parish have in the field of the education and formation of adolescents and youth.

Is not this your age? And do you not often hear it repeated that it is the period in which you must acquire knowledge and prepare well for life? Life is a great gift from God, as we read in the first book of the Bible: "God created man in his own image, in the image of God he created him; male and female he created them" (Gn. 1:27). And of life, which is a divine gift, your present age is certainly the most beautiful, the freshest, the richest in hope, straining as it does towards a joyful and serene future.

Growth, which the Lord gave—together with other commandments—as an order to Adam and Eve, can very well refer to each one of you, and apply to your condition as children and young people. You must grow, that is, develop day by day, and become mature and complete men and women; but—note well—not only in the physical sense, but also and above all in the spiritual sense. It would not suffice to grow only in body (nature itself, moreover, thinks of this); it is necessary to grow especially in spirit, and this is done by exercising those faculties that the Lord—they are others of His gifts—has given to you: intelligence, will, the inclination to love Him and your neighbor.

In this work, none of you is alone: each one finds on his way, in the first place, his parents, who help him, with example, affection and constant attention, in the necessary process of development. Then he also finds the school and the parish. One is geared to your formation, communicating to your minds and hearts the various branches of knowledge which will be valuable in life, and the norms of correct behavior. The other, as a living portion of the Church, is also geared to your formation, to enrich the spirit with those superior goods which are called—do you remember?—divine grace and the virtues of faith, hope and charity. So alongside the family there are two other places, two "Workshops," as it were, in which you can and must see to that complete preparation which, as it corresponds to the will of God the Creator, so it is keenly awaited and desired by all those who are close to you in your youth: parents, teachers and priests.

We read in St. Luke's Gospel that Jesus, in the long years of childhood and youth spent at Nazareth, "increased in wisdom and in stature, and in favor with God and man" (2:52). Just think! Jesus, who was God's own Son, who became a man for us, willed to proceed along the way of gradual development. He, too, willed to correspond to that divine order of growth, and doing so, He left us a marvelous example, which it is our duty to recognize, follow and copy. You, too, beloved sons, must look to Jesus: both in the parish and at school, use your youthful energies to reach a true and positive maturity, completely worthy of your dignity as men and Christians. We are in the period of Lent, which is the time of preparation for Easter, and our Easter—as St. Paul teaches—is Jesus Christ (cf. 1 Cor. 5:7).

To prepare in the best way for your meeting with Him, reflect on the words which, in His name, I have just addressed to you, and strengthen the resolution to "increase in wisdom and in stature, and in favor with God and man" within the parish and school environment, perfecting what you have already received within your families.

"The Trial of Obedience Results in Joy"

On March 12, 1980, the Holy Father addressed the young in St. Peter's Basilica on the difficult but rewarding virtue of obedience.

Beloved young people!

Dear boys and girls!

You have come in large numbers and perhaps also from far away, to Rome, to pray on St. Peter's tomb, to see his Successor and hear his word. I greet you warmly and thank you for your visit, hoping that you will bring back from it to your homes a memory and a sentiment that will be efficacious in your lives.

We are in the liturgical time of Lent, that is, in that particular period of the year, more thoughtful and austere, which brings us day after day to Holy Week and especially to Good Friday, the day that recalls the death of Jesus on the cross for our salvation.

St. Paul, writing to Christians of the city of Philippi, stated: "He humbled himself and became obedient unto death, even death on a cross" (Phil. 2:8). He humbled Himself; He became obedient: they are words that do not seem relevant today, especially if said to young people, when there is a whole systematic opposition to obedience, which is presented as a humiliation of one's personality, a defeat of the intelligence and will, abdication of one's own human dignity; and autonomy, revolt, rebellion are preached....

Precisely Jesus, on the contrary, set us the example of obedience unto death on the cross! And so I exhort you to obedience, speaking to you in the name of Jesus!

Certainly, in the society in which we must live, there are some who are unable to command in the right way; and therefore obedience, when it is necessary, must be respectfully critical.

But there are also—and how many there are!—those who are a living lesson of good: excellent fathers and mothers, who love you and wish only to guide you along the right way; schoolmasters, teachers and headmasters who follow you with delicate care; well-balanced and wise priests, anxious only about your real happiness and your salvation; sisters and catechists, dedicated solely to your real formation.... Well, I say to you, listen to them, obey them!

As you well know, all the saints passed through the trial, sometimes even a heroic one, of obedience: such as the Blessed Virgin, such as St. Joseph, who did nothing but obey the voice of God calling them to a sublime, but also disconcerting and mysterious mission.

Why must you obey?

First of all because obedience is necessary in the general framework of Providence. God did not create you by chance, but for a very clear and straightforward purpose: His eternal glory and our happiness. Parents and all those who have responsibilities over us must, in God's name, help us to reach the purpose willed by the Creator.

Furthermore, external obedience also teaches us to obey the inner law of conscience, that is, the will of God expressed in the moral law.

Finally, you must obey also because obedience makes life serene and consoling: when you are obedient at home, at school, at work, you are happier and bring joy to the environment.

And how must you obey?

Lovingly, and also with holy courage, well aware that nearly always, obedience is difficult, costs sacrifice, calls for commitment and sometimes even involves a heroic effort. It is necessary to look to the crucified Jesus! You must also obey trustfully, convinced that God's grace never fails and that then the soul is filled with immense interior joy. The effort of obedience is repaid with continual paschal joy.

Here, beloved in Christ, is the exhortation I wish to make to you while we are living the period of Lent. May the apostolic blessing, which I willingly impart to you, to your parents and to your teachers, help you and always accompany you.

Bring Christian Joy
to All!

After the recitation of the Angelus on March 16, 1980, John Paul II went to the Paul VI Hall where about twelve thousand secondary school students belonging to "Communion and Liberation"—from all over Italy—were waiting for him. They were led by Don Luigi Giussani, Founder of the movement, and also by his assistants, Don Luigi Negri and Don Massimo Camisasca. As is now the custom in their meetings with the Pope, the young people of "Communion and Liberation" sang several songs for him. The Holy Father then delivered the following address to them.

Beloved young people!

This meeting of ours is pervaded with joy. My joy and yours, because we can see one another, and speak to one another; joy that finds, in this fourth Sunday of Lent, its liturgical expression: "Rejoice, Jerusalem, and all of you who love her, gather!" We are welcomed with these words today at the beginning of Holy Mass. Jerusalem, that is, the whole Church, is invited to express her irrepressible joy. For what reason? Because Easter is now near. Christ, man's Redeemer, is present in His Church, in the world, in history, in our midst!

To you, young people of "Communion and Liberation," who have come from all the regions of Italy, even at the cost of considerable sacrifices, I wish to entrust today a commitment and a charge: *Be, now and always, bearers and transmitters of Christian joy!* In giving you this charge, I cannot fail to recall what my Predecessor Paul VI recommended to all young people in his Apostolic Exhortation *Gaudete in Domino,* of May 9, 1975: "We cordially urge you to be attentive to inner appeals which come to you. We urge you to raise up your eyes, your heart, your fresh energies, to the heights, to accept the effort of the soul's yearnings" (VI).

Above all, bear Christian joy in your hearts: joy that springs from faith serenely accepted; intensely explored by means of personal meditation and study of the Word of God and the teaching of the Church; dynamically lived in union with God in Christ, in prayer and in constant practice of the sacraments, especially the Eucharist and Reconciliation; in assimilation of the Gospel message, which is sometimes difficult for our weak human nature, which is not always in harmony with the requirements, exalting indeed but exacting, of the Sermon on the Mount and of the beatitudes. *Noli gaudere in saeculo*—St. Augustine tells us —*gaude in Christo, gaude in verbo eius, gaude in lege eius…. In corde christiano et tranquillitas erit et pax; sed quamdiu vigilat fides nostra; si autem dormit fides nostra, periclitamur* (Do not rejoice in earthly reality, rejoice in Christ, rejoice in His word, rejoice in His law…. There will be peace and tranquility in the Christian heart; but only as long as our faith is watchful; if, however, our faith sleeps, we are in danger. *Enarr, in ps. 93,* 24f.: PL 37, 1212f.).

The danger that the faith of Christians, your faith as young Christians, may have phases of sluggishness, is always constantly present, especially in these periods of deep and far-reaching changes in the cultural, social, political and economic fields.

But you, beloved young people, are certainly not afraid, far less ashamed, to be, and to show that you are, Christians, always and everywhere!

Bring Christian joy to the environment in which you live normally, that is, to your families, your associations, but especially to *the scholastic world!*

With what hope, what respect, but also what trepidation the citizens of a well-ordered state look to the school, the place in which the young, gathered together, can passionately seek the truth together and make of all the different knowledge acquired a unified synthesis, which will give them the capacity of judging and interpreting the various and complex socio-cultural phenomena.

Unfortunately—it is a complaint that we hear repeated very often—the modern school is going through a crisis and, sometimes, it gives mistaken information and a bad education; while the modern media of social communication, on their part, disseminate from their "chairs" their "lessons" of hedonism, indifferentism, and materialism, and try to win over and subjugate the young particularly.

May your presence in the world of the school, and in the wider one of culture, inspire real interests in the sphere of the various branches of knowledge, in respect for pluralism, but in the firm conviction that culture must aim at the complete perfection of the human being and the real good of the community and of the whole of human society.

Live in close union with the men of your time; try to penetrate into their way of thinking and feeling; succeed in harmonizing the knowledge of science, culture and the most recent discoveries with morality and Christian thought (cf. *Gaudium et spes,* no. 62).

Commit yourselves, young people of "Communion and Liberation," with your study, your preparation, your earnestness, your enthusiasm and your example, to sustaining the faith of your fellow students. This will be a highly meritorious work before God and the Church.

Speaking of Christian joy, which springs from faith and from sincere pursuit of truth, we cannot forget that it is closely connected with love. He who possesses and trans-mits Christian joy is, at the same time, the bearer of a message of solidarity, peace and love! At this point my appeal is intense and pressing. The spiral of violence continues, barbarously and cynically, to cause and sow hatred and death! In this situation, a dramatic one in itself, the most shocking aspect for all men of goodwill is the horrifying fact that young people are killing other young people! Dominated and enslaved by aberrant ideologies, some young people are under the illusion that it is only by killing that this society can be changed. But it is necessary to proclaim with forcefulness and conviction that a world of justice, solidarity and peace, cannot be constructed on blood and on the corpses of victims, whose only crime is to have different views.

Answer blind violence and inhuman hatred, beloved young people, with the impelling power of love! Bear witness with your behavior, with your lives, particularly at school, that ideas are not imposed, but are proposed; that real cultural pluralism, so exalted by modern society, calls for the utmost respect with regard to the ideas of others. On these foundations, construct, day by day, your present, which prepares and is a prelude to your future, of which you are already beginning to be real protagonists.

On your return to your regions, to your homes, to your classrooms, be bearers of these indications and these concerns of the Pope, who, on behalf of the Church, tells you of his understanding, his affection, his esteem and his hope.

May the singing, which always brings life and inspiration to your community assemblies, be the sign of your deep faith in Christ and in the Church.

"Cantate vocibus"—it is again St. Augustine who speaks —*"cantate cordibus, cantate oribus, cantate moribus!"* (Sing with your voice, sing with your heart, sing with your mouth, sing with your whole life!) (*Serm. 34,* cap. 3,6: PL 38,211).

With this renewed invitation to joy, which opens into song, I willingly impart to you my apostolic blessing.

"Be Dynamic Witnesses to the Easter Message"

On March 19, 1980, Pope John Paul II spoke to the boys and girls present in St. Peter's Basilica.

Beloved young people, boys and girls,

I bid you a very hearty welcome, and I tell you at once that I am really happy to be with you, who come from the most varied parishes, schools and associations. Since our meeting takes place on the day of the liturgical solemnity of St. Joseph, I take advantage of the fact to recall to you the silent but important figure of this saint, who was beside Mary and Jesus for so many years and is venerated as patron saint of the Church. Therefore, I am happy to express my most cordial wishes to those of you who bear his name.

Dear young people, I have already said on other occasions, and I wish to repeat again, that you are the hope not only of the world, but above all, of the Church and of the Pope in particular. Your youth, in fact, is rich in promises, as a tree in blossom in spring already promises abundance of fruit for the following seasons. That is why, in your presence, one cannot but be confident, and wait with patience but with certainty, for the full maturation of the many potentialities placed in you both by ordinary human nature and by the Spirit who made you Christians, at Baptism.

The important thing is that you should not disappoint these ardent, and sometimes anxious expectations of both civil and ecclesial society, which likes to see in you not only the repetition of itself but also, and above all, the realization of its own improvement, not only by means of the correction of what has been sown badly, but especially by means of the tenacious continuation of everything initiated in good.

Remember the words of St. Paul to the Ephesians: "Christ loved the church and gave himself up for her...that he might present the church to himself in splendor, without spot or wrinkle or any such thing, that she might be holy and without blemish" (Eph. 5:25, 27). Unlike what happens to any individual living on this earth, this must happen to the Church: that is, that the more time passes and the centuries follow one another, she, instead of growing old, must become younger and younger, in order to be more and more on a level with her eternally young Bridegroom, Jesus Christ, who, "being raised from the dead, will never die again" (Rom. 6:9), but is always "the same yesterday and today and for ever" (Heb. 13:8).

Beloved young people, if you do not put yourselves under the sign of this communion with the Lord, what will become of your lives? You would run the risk of building them on sand, instead of on rock! What sense, indeed could they have, and what joy could you witness to, if you are not united with the One who, according to the Bible, "gives joy to my youth" (Ps. 43:4, LXX) and makes "all things new"? (Rv. 21:5)

You know that, in these days, we are now near to celebrating the solemnity of Easter. You are certainly preparing in a way of faith and conversion for this feast, which is the greatest one of the whole liturgical year. On my part, I urge you to act in such a way that not just one day in the year, but your whole life will be a real Easter, as St. Paul exhorts us: "Christ, our paschal lamb, has been sacrificed! Let us, therefore, celebrate the festival, not with the old leaven, the leaven of malice and evil, but with the unleavened bread of sincerity and truth" (1 Cor. 5:7-8).

Therefore, let your life be really the life of persons risen again with Christ and of dynamic witnesses to His exalting message to the whole world. With Him, indeed, you will really know thoroughly what it means to love men so much as to give your life for them (cf. Mk. 10:45; Jn. 3:16), what it means to promote complete peace and progress, what it means to live in the light coming from the "Son of righteousness" (Mal. 4:2), which is precisely the risen Christ. And you will also know that this height of virtue and this happy youth is not reached and is not maintained without the austere experience of the cross; and the latter, to those who accept it with faith, turns out to be the great value that kindles your enthusiasms, verifies them and, in a word, exalts and strengthens them.

I wish you this whole-heartedly and I also pray to the Lord for this. May my blessing be a token of His fruitful grace, as well as of my fatherly benevolence.

March in the Sign
of Christ

After his address to the young people in St. Peter's Basilica on March 19, 1980, John Paul II lit and blessed the Benedictine torch which was carried by 105 torch-bearers from Norcia, Subiaco and Monte Cassino, through the places principally associated with St. Benedict and Saint Scholastica. The torch arrived in Norcia on the following Saturday evening.

I now wish to address a special greeting to the thousand young torch-bearers of the diocese of Norcia and Spoleto, and of the Abbeys of Subiaco and Monte Cassino, who, together with many relatives and friends of various schools, as well as of the Italian Sporting Center, have come here to have the Benedictine Torch lit and blessed by the Pope. It will then be carried by the same athletes, through the above-mentioned cities, to Norcia, the birthplace of Saint Benedict, to recall the XV centenary of the birth of the great Patriarch of the West and of St. Scholastica, his sister.

Beloved young people, while you carry this torch, spreading its light, remember what luminous cultural and spiritual traditions Umbria has inherited and guards, and be proud of them! Carry out your march in the sign of Christ

Lumen gentium! May this torch bring forth sentiments of brotherhood, concord, and above all Christian solidarity for those who are still suffering as a result of the devastations of the earthquake in your land.

Blessing your torch now, I extend my greeting and good wishes to all those who join you in the name of the Lord, looking forward to the joy of the meeting that I will have with your beloved region next Sunday.

Be Apostles
of Love

About 5:00 p.m. in the afternoon of March 23, 1980, the Holy Father met a very large number of young people in St. Benedict's Square in Norcia. With the young people of Norcia, and those of the other towns of Valnerina stricken by the earthquake, there were various groups from different regions of Italy, who were among the first to bring aid to the people immediately after the earthquake. John Paul II delivered the following address.

Beloved young people,

Now, at the conclusion of this day, so intense and rich in deep emotions and interior joy, I am happy to meet you, young people of Valnerina and the whole of Umbria, together with those of you who have gathered here to strengthen your spirit in that generous dedication that you jointly displayed immediately after the disastrous earthquake which struck these hard-working people last year. You bore at that time a luminous witness, all the more to be appreciated because it was a spontaneous expression springing from your dynamic and serene spirit of sacrifice and emulating, in the work of assistance and solidarity, the example of precocious maturity offered by the young Benedict, whose mind—as St. Gregory the Pope says—matured from childhood, anticipating age with virtues (cf. *Dialogues*, II, Prol.).

Inspired by such a resolution to cooperate in the good of the community and especially of those living in painful conditions of hardship, you set yourselves in the true light of the "Christian humanism" proposed and lived by the Saint of Norcia, and which can be summed up in true respect for man in every expression of his value, in efficacious love for him, especially when he reveals the countenance and the voice of suffering.

Accept, therefore, dear young people of Caritas, Agesci, the Community of St. Giles, Communion and Liberation, the Focolare, Catholic Action and the various ecclesial groups, my affectionate greeting in this birthplace of St. Benedict and, above all, my congratulations on what you have carried out with youthful enthusiasm.

Your commitment of charity and altruism has found its place in the age-old course of the Benedictine message. The latter is valid and relevant today also, because it is firmly attached to perennial values, which, if they require ever new expression and verification, are such as to vivify and elevate the human experience of all times. This message must attract and win over also the young people of the present generation, who are often disappointed and confused in the maze of a hedonistic and permissive society.

In fact, the sad times in which St. Benedict's spiritual experience found its place, were also full of deep contradictions, ambiguous and utopian aspirations, vain resolutions of grandeur; those times, too, were marked by desolate moral wretchedness, and very low living standards, under the impact of peoples in expansion, but still dominated by promptings of violence. The Saint of Norcia, however, nourished by the certainties of the Faith, reasserted the power of a Christianity that taught moral dignity and spiritual freedom, and was at the same time the architect of civilization.

As you have clearly experienced, the conquest of interior spaces that offer God His rightful place in the human spirit, all that commitment, in a word, which we could distinguish with the primacy of "ORA," "pray," is absolutely not in conflict, but on the contrary brings relief and grants creative intuition to true openness to the social sphere, to daily duty deeply felt, to the living forces of work and culture; thus animating with fervent inspiration and spirit of service the great and agitated world of "WORK."

What can I say to you in particular in this picturesque setting of crags and valleys which tempered the strong and courageous spirit of the predestined youth, and at a moment so charged with brotherhood and communion pervaded by the spiritual presence of the Father of our European civilization?

Continue, dear young people, with the witness you generously bear, because, while it is in harmony with the values of Benedictine tradition, it is at the same time faithful to modern men, interpreting their deepest aspirations.

Importance of Silence and Meditation

You have felt the urgent need of meeting the Absolute and, therefore, you have discovered the importance of interiority, silence and meditation, to be able to grasp the definitive and reconciling meaning of your own existence. You have tasted the sweetness of prayer and of that ever renewed and persevering reconciliation of friendship with the Lord established in hearts by an existential attitude of humble and active obedience to the heavenly Father. With St. Benedict, then, I will address to you the fatherly invitation: *"Ausculta, fili, verba magistri";* listen, sons, to the teachings of true teachers, and make your hearts attentive in prayerful silence, in order to return, through the effort of docile obedience to wholesome precepts, to Him, from whom a position of indolence or rebellion takes us away (cf. *Rule,* Prol.). Place yourselves often before the interior Master, and those who represent Him, in the attitude of the true disciple, who knows how to be silent and listen.

Premises for Complete Human Revival

You, dear young people, have discovered charity and love, which are manifested in solicitude for your neighbor and in an open dialogue with brothers, respecting their dignity and being available for a diffusion of reciprocal contribution. They are values that St. Benedict established—in a socio-economic context in which exploitation and arbitrary action predominated—by opposing the spirit of brotherhood to violence, and industrious commitment to sloth, in order to lay down the premises for a complete human revival.

The Benedictine monastery will be almost a forerunner of the new *societas;* within its walls discriminations between nobles and plebeians, between rich and poor, between free men and slaves, are canceled. In it persecuted settlers and barbarian oppressors will find refuge, setting aside, before God, old rivalries and recent rancor, in order to dedicate themselves to prayer, work and mutual support. The Saint, full of delicacy in treating the monks, in welcoming the pilgrims, in looking after the sick, lists among the means to act rightly: *"Pauperes recreare,...infirmum visitare,...in tribulatione subvenire, dolentem consolari;... nihil amori Christi praeponere;* help the poor,...visit the sick,...assist those who are victims of misfortune,... console the afflicted,...put nothing before love of Christ" *(Rule,* Chap. IV).

Violence Born of Hate

You love beauty which is the splendor of order and, therefore, mainly innocence of life and harmony of the spirit. The Rule, on the writing of which the Saint was engaged for a long time, and which indicates with wisdom and moderation the ways and the times of prayer and work, shows the importance he attached to this beauty emerging from an orderly rhythm of life. He harmonizes, indeed, in himself, the sense of authority, order and discipline, borrowed from the classical world, with a delicacy of spirit that matured during his long progress towards perfection.

It is the order, primarily of a spiritual nature, that reigns there which enables the monasteries to be great centers of life and creative activity in the mature awareness that Christianity is, at the same time, asceticism in regard to God and also earthly commitment, so that prayer leads to work not only as a means of ensuring monks the necessary maintenance, but also as a most valuable opportunity for personal discipline and social advancement.

The powerful call of the Benedictine message to seek God and His will, to establish a social context permeated by brotherhood and order, takes on an extraordinarily topical note on this day of prayer and reflection, in regard to the very serious problem of terrorism in Italy.

The violence that is upsetting the social fabric of the Italian nation is not fortuitous: It is based on a precise program, it is born of the spirit of hate. The origin of violence is here, only here. People must not let themselves be deceived by other motivations. That is why it is so necessary for Christians to be able to discern this spirit, understand its intrinsic perversion (cf. Jn. 3:15), and not let themselves be contaminated so that they can withdraw themselves from the spiral of hate and not let themselves be taken in by its promptings. On the contrary, be clear-sighted and generous apostles of love.

Dear young people, you have picked out the ideal and main values of St. Benedict's witness and, with the grace of God, you have undertaken to put them into practice in your lives. Continue to interpret them and embody them with courage, generosity and enthusiasm, convinced that the Lord Himself is the only Guarantor, as the Psalmist says, of a building with solid foundations, and therefore of a just and human future, a peaceful and productive society, and harmonious and brotherly order. With my affectionate blessing.

"A Radiant Reflection of Jesus Christ"

During the general audience of March 26, 1980, Pope John Paul II urged the young people present to incarnate the Paschal Mystery in their own lives.

And now a word to the young. Welcome, beloved in Christ! Your presence, so joyful and spontaneous, bears witness that the Church is young and projected towards the future. Be aware of your responsibilities: The message of Christ is entrusted to your generosity and your enthusiasm. You will have to take it into the new millennium, which is appearing on the horizon. It is an exacting message: It proclaims redemption by means of the cross; life and joy through suffering and death. It proclaims Christ crucified, who died and rose again.

If you wish to be credible witnesses to it, make an effort above all to incarnate it in your lives. Those who approach you must be able to gather in your words, in your acts, in everything that you are, a reflection of the luminous face of the risen Christ. Jesus wishes to walk with you along the ways of the world, which is being constructed in these difficult years: Do not forget it! I give you my apostolic blessing.

The Savior Approaches and Beckons to You

In the afternoon of April 9, 1980, the Holy Father concelebrated the Mass for participants in the international pilgrimage of Mass-servers. John Paul II delivered the following homily.

Dear friends,

I am happy to celebrate the Eucharist surrounded by all of you—children, young people and adults. In the various countries of Europe that you come from, you usually carry out this service around your priests, or your bishops, who are the successors of the Apostles. And this afternoon, around the Bishop of Rome, who is the Successor of Peter, the Pastor given by Christ to His disciples as a whole.

You have come here to take part in the paschal joy of the Church, which is celebrating the resurrection of the Lord with Christians of all countries. But you yourselves bear this joy of Easter within you. Not only do you believe in the living Jesus, not only have you received His grace within you, but you are also available to serve Christ in the accomplishment of your liturgical service. You experience again, almost continually, this proximity to which the Lord Jesus, especially in this paschal period, invites and admits His disciples, by meeting them and revealing His resurrection to them.

As you know, it was the women, in the first place, who came to His tomb on Easter morning, and Jesus greets and reassures them, asking them to take the news to the Apostles. There is Mary Magdalene who looks for His body and who would like to detain Jesus when He calls her by her name. There are the disciples of Emmaus who walk with Him, ask Him to stay with them and who recognize Him when He breaks the bread. There are the Apostles, and in particular Thomas, to whom the risen Christ shows His hands and His feet and entrusts the Gospel for the whole world. There is Peter and there is James. (Again, the Apostles perceive Him in the course of their laborious fishing and Jesus welcomes them at His meal by the side of the lake. He appears before five hundred disciples, as St. Paul, the convert, says.) Jesus brought them all into full faith, to the extent that they could say like Thomas: "My Lord and my God." He prepared them to live continually in His invisible presence, in peace and joy. He gave them His Spirit. He made them His witnesses in the eyes of others. In short, He brought them into His intimate and glorious life.

Today, the same Lord Jesus, raised to heaven, is present and acts in the sacraments of the Church, especially in the Eucharist. And you, associated in the liturgical service of the altar, have the honor and the happiness to approach this Christ intimately.

Love Is the Sign

The liturgy, it is true, does not fill the whole activity of the Church. There is a very large part of proclamation, catechesis, and preaching, to awaken faith, nourish it and educate it. And you yourselves benefit from it. There is personal prayer, in which each one must speak to the Lord in secrecy, or with his friends. There are all the works of the apostolate and of charity: Love is the sign by which Christ's disciples are recognized. But the liturgy is the summit towards which the whole action of the Church tends, and the source from which all her strength flows (cf. Constitution *Sacrosanctum concilium,* nos. 9-10).

It is there that the covenant with God is established, that the people are sanctified, glorify God, draw closer their ties with the Church and strengthen their charity. During and since the great Second Vatican Council, the Church has wished to renew the liturgy, so that it may express these holy realities more clearly and that the Christian people may take part in it through a full, active and community celebration (cf. *ibid.,* no. 21). This celebration, even in its simplicity, must always be beautiful and dignified, and it must lead participants to enter the holy action of Jesus who lets us hear His word, offers Himself in sacrifice and unites us with His body.

On the occasion of Holy Thursday, I myself have just written a letter to all the bishops and, through them, to all the priests, on the meaning of the Eucharist and the way of celebrating it.

An Office To Perform

With regard to you, my dear young friends, you carry out beside the priest, who alone acts in the name of Christ, a service which has the purpose of making the greatness of the Eucharistic Mystery even clearer. Listen to what the bishops said in this connection at the last Council: "In liturgical celebrations, each person, minister or layman, who has an office to perform, should carry out all and only those parts which pertain to his office by the nature of the rite and the norms of the liturgy. Servers—here you, too, are named—readers, commentators and members of the choir also exercise a genuine liturgical function. They ought, therefore, to discharge their offices with the sincere piety and decorum demanded by so exalted a ministry and rightly expected of them by God's people" *(Sacrosanctum concilium,* nos. 28 and 29). In my recent letter On the Mystery and Worship of the Holy Eucharist, I added: "The possibilities that the post-conciliar renewal has introduced in this respect are indeed often utilized so as to make us witnesses of and sharers in the authentic celebration of the Word of God. There is also an increase in the number of people taking an active part in this celebration" (no. 10).

This applies particularly also to the altar boys, servers, the *Messdiener, Ministranten, servants, chierichetti, enfants de choeur, grands clercs,* as they are called in other countries. They accompany the priest to the altar, pray at his side, and hand to him what he needs for the Holy Sacrifice. In a word, they carry out almost the functions of acolytes, without having received that ministry.

There are other services, moreover, which are likewise necessary for a worthy celebration of the Eucharist. I am thinking of the service of "readers," which concerns particularly the older ones among you; of the service of "choristers," especially in the framework of the *schola cantorum,* the church choirs for children, young people and adults. These services are the task of the whole community and, therefore, of laymen and women. When they are carried out properly, the whole celebration becomes more expressive, and there is deeper participation among the faithful. Reference could also be made to those who take part in the procession of gifts: the gifts are, in a way, a symbol of everything that the community brings at the celebration of the Eucharist as a sacrifice to God and a spiritual offering; among them are bread and wine, which become the body and the blood of the Lord.

My dear young friends, all these services must, however, be well prepared. You must endeavor to understand the liturgy, even more, you must bear witness to Christ and the Church in many ways. To do this and to learn this is the educational task of your groups, in which you dedicate yourselves to prayer and to the apostolate. Those who have the task of reading or singing the texts of Holy Scripture must understand well the meaning of the Word of God, meditate upon it and learn to proclaim it in a worthy and clear way, so that it is heard and understood properly, to the spiritual advantage of those present.

In this connection I would like to request urgently that priests and educators should devote all the necessary care and time to this preparation.

It is my earnest wish that the liturgy should be restored everywhere in all its dignity and be carried out as a really holy action, because it puts us in communion with Christ, in His threefold holiness! I would like the congregation to take part in it actively, full of faith and awe, in a meditative and devout spirit and also with due zeal. You have the opportunity to contribute to this to a great extent. I know, too, that many people in your country endeavor to do so. Unfortunately, however, this service also seems to be neglected in many places. Under the pretext of simplicity, celebrations become monotonous or run the risk of losing their sacred and solemn character. I, for my part, have had unforgettable experiences in Poland, particularly in my diocese, Krakow, in which the young contributed a decisive part to the beauty and vitality of the Eucharistic Celebration.

Listen to the Lord Who Speaks

Let us now return to the Gospel of this day. It is in a way the fabric of each of our Masses. Like the disciples of

Emmaus, we listen to the Lord who speaks to us of the meaning of His death, His resurrection, and what He expects from us. The celebrant, like Jesus, explains it to you. But that is not enough. The Lord, in the person of His minister, blesses and breaks the bread. Under the appearance of the bread, your eyes, educated by faith, are sure to recognize Him. This recognition, this closeness of Jesus, and even more the fact that you yourselves receive, after a worthy preparation, this Bread of Life which is His body, fill you with unspeakable joy, because you love the Lord. I hope that this experience, which you frequently renew beside the celebrant, will leave lasting traces in your lives. Certainly, you are not dispensed from effort, because there is the risk that you may become "accustomed" to these gestures which you see so close at hand and so often; and that you may not recognize sufficiently the love of your Savior who approaches and beckons to you. Your heart must keep watch, prayer must maintain in you the desire to meet Him, and after Mass you must also share the love received with others.

Your service, dear friends, associates you, therefore, with the sacred ministry of the priest who celebrates the Eucharist and the other sacraments, in Christ's own name. But will you always have among you the priests that you desire and whom the People of God cannot do without? You know how much your countries need priestly vocations. Addressing the boys and youths who are present, I say to them: And you, have you ever thought that the Lord Jesus was inviting you, perhaps, to greater intimacy with Him—to a higher service, to a radical donation, precisely as His priest, His minister? What grace it would be for you, for your family, for your parish, for the Christian communities that are waiting for priests! Certainly, this grace is not an obligation.... "If you are willing," Jesus said. But so many youths—even today—still have a taste for risk! I am sure that many of them are capable of leaving everything to follow Jesus and continue His mission. In any case, you must ask yourself the question loyally. The way in which you carry out your service now prepares you to answer the Lord's call.

Walk with Jesus

During the general audience of April 19, 1980, the Holy Father addressed a special plea to the young to journey through life with Jesus.

The numerous groups of young people and children present here deserve a special greeting today. To you, dear boys and girls, who are in the bloom of life, I express the cordial wish that you may carry out the whole journey of life with the same fortune as the two wayfarers going to Emmaus. I exhort you to be witnesses to paschal joy and to the resurrection of Christ along the roads of the world, in your families, in your cities, in your environments of study and play. I bless you all willingly.

"Society Is Waiting, Christ Is Waiting"

Pope John Paul II's farewell address in Turin, on April 13, 1980, was delivered in front of the Church of the Great Mother of God, which overlooks the huge Piazza Vittorio. The following is his impassioned plea to the youth of the city.

Young people, young people—I am speaking to you—do not let yourselves be influenced! Be generous and good! Society and the Church, your country, need you: *"Quid hic statis tota die otiosi?* Why do you stand here idle all day?" I repeat to you with the words of the Gospel (Mt. 20:6). Social works and works of animation in the field of youth, the missions, culture and sports are waiting for your contribution, too! The Church is waiting. Society is waiting! Christ is waiting! Do not disappoint this common hope of ours! Do not disappoint my hope!

Christianity Crowns Your Personality

On April 13, 1980, after meeting with the religious sisters in the Church of Maria Ausiliatrice in the afternoon, John Paul II went out into the large square in front of the basilica, and from a specially erected platform in front of the statue of St. John Bosco, he gave the following address to the thousands of young people who had come to greet him.

Beloved young people of the city and of the Church in Turin, could there fail to be a special appointment with you on the occasion of this visit of mine? Yes or no?

(Crowd: No!)

So here we have a fixed point. We must thank the organizers who made provision for this appointment and this program.

Finding myself in your land, I felt, more than the opportuneness, the necessity of addressing to you my word of exhortation and incentive, also to strengthen the hope of all those who, in the difficult years that we are living, turn to you with renewed confidence.

Turin is a city which has remarkable and literally exemplary traditions in the religious-educational field. It presents to us chosen figures of men and youths who, though they lived in different periods from ours, are surprisingly relevant today, and can offer the modern world very precious lessons. Among the many names that I could mention, I will select only two.

The first is that of St. John Bosco, who was a great educator of the young, to the extent that his work on their behalf has had a far-reaching influence not only here and in the surrounding region, but also in Italy and in the world. What can I say of my Krakow, of my Poland? There are so many Salesians! I was in a Salesian parish for several years. So I cannot fail to speak about St. John Bosco.

I would like to ask, then: what does it mean to be a great educator? It means, first of all, being a man who is able "to understand" the young. And, in fact, we know that Don Bosco had special insight into young souls. He was always ready to listen attentively and to understand the youths who flocked in large numbers to him in the youth club of Valdocco and in the Church of Our Lady Help of Christians. But it must be added at once that the reason for this peculiar depth in "understanding" the young was that he "loved" them just as deeply.

To understand and to love: Here we have the un-equaled pedagogical formula of Don Bosco, who—I think—if he were in your midst today, with his mature experience as an educator and with the common sense of the genuine Piedmontese, would be able to pick out and distinguish clearly in you the echo, never extinguished, of the words that Christ addresses to those who wish to be His disciples: "Come, follow me" (Mt. 19:21; Lk. 18:22). *Follow me* with faithfulness and constancy; *follow me* right from this moment; *follow me* along the various, possible ways of your life! The whole action of St. John Bosco—it seems to me—can be summed up and defined in this successful and masterly "start" of the young on their way to Christ.

The second name is that of Pier Giorgio Frassati, a figure nearer to our own age (he died, in fact, in 1925). He shows us in real life what it really means for a young lay-man to give a concrete answer to the "come, follow me."

Even a rapid glance at his life, consummated in the span of barely twenty-four years, is enough to understand what was the answer that Pier Giorgio gave to Jesus Christ. It was that of a "modern" young man, open to the problems of culture, sports (he was a good mountaineer), to social questions, to the real values of life. At the same time it was that of a deep believer, nourished on the Gospel message, of a staunch, consistent character passionately eager to serve brothers and consumed by burning charity which led him to approach, in an order of absolute precedence, the poor and the sick.

Two Outstanding Models for Youth

Why, speaking to you now, did I wish to take an example from these two figures? Because they serve to show, in a certain sense from two different aspects, what is essential for the Christian view of man. Both of them—Don Bosco as a true Christian educator and Pier Giorgio as a genuine young Christian—indicate to us that what counts most in this view is the person and his vocation, as was established by God. You know very well that this reference to the person is now a frequent one on my part, because it is really a question of a fundamental element, which can never be disregarded. When I say person, I do not intend to speak of an autonomous humanism, limited to the realities of this earth. Man—it is worth recalling—is of immense value in himself, but he does not have it from himself, because he has received it from God, by whom he was created "in his image and likeness" (Gn. 1:26, 27). There is no adequate definition of man but this one! This value is like a "talent" and, according to the teaching of the well-known parable (Mt. 25:14-30), it must be used well, that is, used in such a way that it will bear fruit abundantly. Here, young people, is the

Christian view of man, which, starting from God the Creator and Father, reveals the person in what he is and in what he should be.

Fruit for Eternity

I spoke of bearing fruit, and here, too, the Gospel helps me, when it proposes—it is a reading that we have met with recently in the sacred liturgy—the metaphor of the barren fig tree, which runs the risk of being uprooted (Lk. 13:6-9). Man must bear fruit *in time*, that is, during his earthly life, and not only for himself, but also for others, for the society of which he is an integral part. However, this activity of his in time, precisely because he is "contained" in time, must not make him forget or neglect his other essential dimension, that of a being directed towards eternity. Man, therefore, must bear fruit, at the same time, also *for eternity*.

If we deprive man of this perspective, he will remain a barren fig tree.

On the one hand, he must "fill time with himself" in a creative way, because the ultra-terrestial dimension certainly does not dispense him from having to act in a responsible and genuine way, taking part effectively and in collaboration with all other men in the building up of society according to the concrete requirements of the historical moment, in which his life is cast. This is the Christian sense of man's "historicity."

On the other hand, this commitment of faith plunges the young into a contemporary dimension which brings with it, in a sense, a view that is contrary to Christianity. This anti-view presents the following characteristics, which I recall, though in summary fashion. The man of today often lacks the sense of the transcendental, of supernatural realities, of something that is beyond him. Man cannot live without something that goes further, that is beyond him. Man lives his life if he is aware of this, if he must always go beyond himself, transcend himself. This transcendence is deeply inscribed in the human constitution of the person. Now, in the contemporary anti-view, as I said, the meaning of man's existence is, therefore, "determined" within a materialistic conception with regard to the various problems, such as, for exampie: justice, work, etc.; hence, those multiform conflicts between social categories or nations, in which the various collective forms of egoism are manifested.

It is necessary, on the contrary, to go beyond this closed conception, fundamentally an alienating one, opposing to it that wider horizon of which sound reason itself and, still more so, the Christian faith, give us a glimpse. There, in fact, problems find a fuller solution; there, justice assumes completeness and implementation in all its aspects; there, human relations, with every form of selfishness excluded, correspond to the dignity of man, as a person on whom God's face shines.

Choosing with Christ

All this shows the importance of that choice which you young people must make! Make it *with Christ,* following Him courageously and adhering to His teaching, aware of the eternal love which found in Him its supreme expression and its definitive witness. In telling you this, I certainly cannot ignore the obstacles and the dangers—unfortunately neither slight nor infrequent—that you meet with in the various environments of today's social context. But you must not let yourselves be turned aside: you must never yield to the temptation, a subtie one and, therefore, all the more insidious, of thinking that this choice may contradict the formation of your personality.

I do not hesitate to affirm that this opinion is completely false: to consider that human life, in the process of its growth and maturation, may be "diminished" by the influence of faith in Christ, is an idea to be rejected. Exactly the opposite is true: just as civilization would be impoverished and mutilated without the presence of the religious element, of the Christian element, so the life of the individual man and particularly of the young person, would be incomplete without a strong experience of faith, drawn from direct contact with the crucified and risen Christ.

Christianity, the faith, believe me, young people, completes and crowns your personality. Centered as it is on the figure of Christ, true God and true Man and, as such, Redeemer of man, it opens you to consideration, understanding and enjoyment of everything great, beautiful and noble in the world and in man. Adherence to Christ does not repress, but expands and exalts the "drives" with which the wisdom of God the Creator has endowed you. Adherence to Christ does not mortify, but strengthens the sense of moral duty, giving you the desire and the satisfaction of committing yourselves for "something really worthwhile."

Source of Real Joy

It gives you, I repeat, the desire and the satisfaction of committing yourselves in this way, and preserving the spirit against the tendencies that not infrequently make themselves felt in the spirit of the young, to "let themselves go" either in the direction of an irresponsible and lazy abdication, or along the way of blind and murderous violence. Above all—always remember this—adherence to Christ will be the source of real joy, deep joy. I repeat to you, adherence to Christ is the source of a joy that the world cannot give and that—as He Himself announced to His disciples—no one can ever take from you (cf. Jn. 16:22), even while you are in the world.

This joy, as the fruit of a paschal faith and—as I said this morning—the fruit "of contact" with Christ, as the ineffable gift of His Spirit, is intended as the point of arrival of my talk to you today. I want to arrive at this word "joy." I want to arrive at this word, because we are living the paschal week. *Christianity is joy,* and those who profess it and let it shine through their own lives, have the duty of bearing witness to it, communicating it and spreading it around them. That is why I mentioned these two figures. Don Bosco: I went again to visit his tomb, and he seemed to me always joyful, always smiling. And Pier Giorgio: he was a young man of joy that swept everything along with it, a joy that also overcame so many difficulties in his life because the period of youth is also always a period of trial of strength.

Love and Freedom

As young people, you are preparing to construct not only your future, but also that of the future generations. What is to be transmitted to them? You must ask yourselves this question. Only material goods, with the addition, perhaps, of a richer culture, a higher level of scientific knowledge, and a more advanced technology? Or, over and above this, or rather even prior to this, do you not want to transmit that higher perspective which I mentioned, those spiritual goods which are called love and freedom? True love, true freedom, I tell you, because these great words: love and freedom, can easily be exploited. They can easily be exploited.

In our age we are witnesses of a terrible exploitation of these words: love and freedom. The real meaning of these words: love and freedom, must be found again. I tell you, you must return to the Gospel. You must return to the school of Christ. Then you will transmit these spiritual goods: the sense of justice in all human relationships, the promotion and safeguarding of peace. And I tell you again, they are words that have been exploited, exploited many, many times. It is always necessary to return to the school of Christ, to find again the true, full and deep meaning of these words.

The necessary support for these values lies only in the possession of a certain and sincere faith: a faith that embraces God and man, man in God. Where there is God and where there is Jesus Christ, His Son, this foundation is a solid one; it is deep, it is very deep. There is not a more suitable, a deeper dimension to be given to this word "man," to this word "love," to this word "freedom," to these words "peace" and "justice": there is not any other, no other but Christ. Then, always returning to this school, here is the search for those precious gifts that you young people must transmit to future generations, to the world of tomorrow; with Him it will be easier and it cannot but succeed.

As I am about to take leave of you, I wish to raise you to this vision of transcendence and beauty from which your Christian life will acquire solidity and go from strength to strength (Ps. 84:7) and bloom—because you are young, and you must bloom—bloom in works and also for earthly society. Let them be a premise and a promise of a more human and, therefore, more serene future. This is the major imperative of this age of ours, which is becoming sad, and will be even sadder, even more tragic, if it does not see that perspective which only you young people can give to it, to our century, to our generation, to our Italy, to our world!

And now, let us call forward the Cardinals, the bishops. Let us give the blessing to these young people. Let us say a prayer, the Our Father, and then we will give a blessing to all of you present here, the bishops together with the Bishop of Rome, who is a pilgrim in Turin today.

Blessed be Jesus Christ!

Dream of a New World

On April 14, 1980, the Holy Father received over three hundred and fifty girls of Women's Catholic Action of Luxembourg. John Paul II delivered the following address.

Dear girls of Women's Catholic Action of Luxembourg,

The Pope is always very happy to open his house and his heart to everyone, but especially to the young, whom he would like to help, on his part, to take charge of their lives and their future.

Thank you for coming to visit me! And all my best wishes for the full success of your stay in Rome, which is mainly centered on study of a subject that must arouse your enthusiasm: "Dream of a new world." Do not dreams and the attraction of the new inhabit the hearts of the young?

Dream, therefore, now and always, of making your life and that of others successful! A life always in search of truth, freedom rightly understood, and above all, continual dedication to others! Such a conception of existence, referred to Christ, who came to give life in abundance, cannot but put you on the way to a real development of your personalities and a noble service of mankind.

You are dreaming of a new world! You are right! This longing for a world increasingly freed of what weighs down spirits and hearts, of what compromises or degrades the internal life of nations or their relations with one another, certainly helps to renew the dynamism of society, which, alas, is more inclined to settle down in comfort than to climb to the peaks. But dream in a realistic way! Only faithfulness to the present, in fact, will deliver you from the fear or disappointments of the future. This exacting faithfulness is necessarily incarnated in the daily pursuit of a solid human formation and, for you young Christian women, in belonging to Jesus Christ in a more and more conscious way.

This faithfulness will involve marvelous moments and bursts of enthusiasm, but also difficulties in relationships with others, and with regard to the academic trend, professional integration, the environment of permissiveness or skepticism, and temptations of all kinds. But never doubt your capacities or the power of Jesus Christ which accompanies your faithfulness in a mysterious but real way.

Dear young people, the liturgical period of Easter brings precisely—for you as for all baptized people aware of their baptism—special and very precious grace! The grace of increasing your certainty that the Christ who died and rose again, if accepted in faith, makes you capable, today and where you are living, of overcoming the obstacles to the coming of a new world in you and around you!

I bless you with all my heart, as well as your dear country, Luxembourg.

Rooted in Faith, Be Witnesses to Jesus Christ

On April 14, 1980, the Holy Father received in audience a numerous group of young people from the Archdiocese of Rouen. John Paul II delivered the following address.

Dear friends,

I am happy to meet you, as I like to meet young Christians whenever my timetable permits, to witness their human and religious vitality and encourage their faith. Jesus said to Peter: "Strengthen your brothers." This is what I am doing this morning, in union with your Archbishop, your chaplains, the sisters and lay men and women who bring you their help and whom I congratulate. The evangelization of the young remains an important part of our ministry.

I leave you two simple instructions. On the one hand, *take root in faith, in the faith of the Church.* It is a question for you of accepting the message of Christ—which cannot be invented; of grafting your life onto His, of entering with Him into a personal relationship with the Father, with your brothers, of reproducing His way of loving. We cannot learn that from the world, in any case, not from the world that doubts or does not believe, or lets itself be guided solely by its impressions and immediate pleasure. Moments of reflection, of prayer, are necessary among Christians, with the chaplain, at school and in the parish, round the Word of God and the sacraments; the rich sap that comes to us from Jesus, through the Apostles Peter and Paul, through saints like Francis and Clare, must be found again. That is what you have tried to do here. That is what you must continue to do. In this way you will strengthen your identity as a Christian, which would otherwise be shaken or impoverished.

On the other hand, you will become, thereby, *witnesses to Christ.* For the world needs to know the Good News through you: through the witness of your faith in Jesus Christ, your attachment to the Church—the Church, a beloved mother!—through your pure and joyful life, completely available to welcome your brothers, to whom you are really able to give your attention, your time and your help. That is the sign by which disciples are recognized.

I think that you are preparing in this way for an adult apostolate, lived if possible in a team. And I hope too that some, won over by Christ and seeing the immense spiritual needs of their brothers, will not hesitate to consecrate themselves completely to Christ's mission. Yes, Christ calls you to follow Him, today as yesterday. I echo His call.

May Christ be your joy and your strength! I bless you from the bottom of my heart, together with your educators in the Faith!

Famine for Hearing the Word of God

At the general audience of April 16, 1980, Pope John Paul II addressed a message to a group of students from the North American College who were to be ordained deacons the following day.

I am pleased to have here today a group of students from the North American College who are to be ordained deacons tomorrow. You will be admitted to a ministry of service to those in need, and the greatest need is to hear God's word: as the prophet Amos said, "not a famine of bread, nor thirst for water, but for hearing the word of the Lord" (Amos 8:11). May God assist you in fulfilling your ministry. May He bless you and all the members of your families.

Give a Christian Sense to Reality

At the same audience the Holy Father encouraged the young people present.

I address an affectionate greeting to all the young people present at this audience, among whom students prevail. To you, who bear in your hearts your hopes and those of the whole world, I wish, in this paschal climate, to address St. Paul's words: "If then you have been raised with Christ, seek the things that are above, where Christ is, seated at the right hand of God" (Col. 3:1).

What does it mean and involve, for you young people, to "seek the things that are above"? It certainly does not mean that you should lose interest in "the things that are below," that is, the problems that concern the practical, everyday life of man. It means, on the contrary, giving a perspective, a "Christian" sense to the whole human reality in which you are involved: to your study, your work, your life in society, your sentimental life, and also your amusement, so that you may always be able to spread the paschal joy that overflows from your hearts.

"You Are the Hope of the Church"

On April 26, 1980, to the group of student representatives of the major seminaries, the Pope spoke as follows.

I address a special affectionate greeting to the group of seminarians, students of theology and representatives of the major seminaries, gathered in these days at Villa Cavalletti, Grottaferrata, to study the subject: "Seminarians and Priestly Vocations." I am grateful to you, beloved sons, for your visit, and I wish to extend my thanks to members of the National Secretariat of Priests and Men and Women Religious for having invited you to the congress, thus enabling you to take part in this meeting.

Great is my joy at seeing you: you are, in fact, the hope of your dioceses and of the whole Church. You have already covered considerable ground on the way to the priesthood: your cultural, theological and spiritual preparation is well underway. Study of the science of God and of His revealed Word, which takes place in the context of other important disciplines, must stimulate more and more your commitment to Christ, the eternal Priest, who has chosen you to be heralds of His Gospel message, dispensers of His grace and of His mysteries. To this lofty dignity there must correspond intense faith, constant prayer, limpidity of thought and morals, generous availability for the expectations of the People of God, and docile submission to the Magisterium of your Pastors, assisted by the Holy Spirit.

Though it should not be too difficult to reach this aim, thanks also to the fatherly solicitude of your superiors and teachers, your ministry will not be an easy one. Like that of Jesus, it must be exercised with deep humility and, above all, with invincible trust in Him who said: *"Vos amici mei estis"* ("You are my friends"—Jn. 15:14). May the knowledge that the Pope is following you with his prayers and his affection be an encouragement to you.

And since we are on the eve of the Sunday dedicated to vocations, I send my affectionate thought to all those who are generously preparing for the priesthood and for religious life, following the divine voice that calls them to give themselves to the Church and to souls.

Besides you, I greet also all the young people present in this Square, appealing to them fervently to reflect on this generous witness, which has just been outlined. It can fully satisfy their courage, their enthusiasm, their ideals of service and advancement, to be undertaken with intrepid faith and without human interests.

With these wishes I invoke the divine assistance on you and on all your dear ones and I willingly impart to you the apostolic blessing.

"Look Beyond the Limits of Time and History"

On April 29, 1980, the Holy Father received in audience the members of the Management and General Councils of the Youth Initiative Center, led by President Giuseppe Lepore. In the course of a ceremony that took place on April 28, representatives of the Center had awarded "The Oscar of the Young, 1979" to Cardinal Bernardin Gantin, President of the Pontifical Commission Iustitia et Pax *and of the Pontifical Council* Cor unum, *to bear witness to their own support and esteem for the activity carried out by the Church on behalf of peace in the world.*

Pope John Paul II delivered the following address.

Gentlemen and dear young people:

My joyful welcome to you who belong to the Management and General Councils of the Youth Initiative Center, and have wished to meet the Pope to receive a word of support and guidance for your exemplary and dynamic initiatives. You propose to foster among persons of your own age enlightened and responsible participation in the solution of problems concerning culture, politics, art and in general the life of society, to promote the fundamental values of justice and peace. To you present here and to all your friends and colleagues, equally anxious to cooperate in the construction of a world more and more animated by ideals of Christian inspiration, goes my affectionate greeting, charged with hope, which is projected into the distance, towards the future that you will be called to construct with commitment, and which I hope will be active and serene.

In the framework of your programs and as a proof of your eager presence you have wished to award "The Oscar of the Young" for the year 1979 to an ecclesiastical personality who, owing to his office, represents in an outstanding and significant way the concern of the Catholic Church in the humanitarian field and for the cause of peace in the world.

The Vicar of Christ thanks you for the appreciation and the consideration you show for the beneficial work of the Church within present-day society. The Church, in fact, though it has the primary mission of directing man towards the supernatural and ultra-terrestrial purposes that constitute the essential content of her message, never forgets the concrete, earthly situation of civil society, and, while she endeavors to animate it interiorly with the values of charity and collaboration, assumes at the same time and shares its burdens, hardships and sufferings.

Interior liberation, observance of the law of love that puts man in the service of man, justice which distributes with wisdom and impartiality, respect for the commandment of forgiveness which extinguishes the thirst for vengeance and smothers hatred, are as many aims of the kingdom of God on earth, which the believer in Christ is called to establish and to radicate in the context of his own individual and social responsibility. In this way, evangelization and advancement proceed at the same rate, and one sustains the other, the former offering ideal motivations and the latter being its convincing and effective manifestation.

Dear young people, make an effort, then, to get to know better and better, with the insight of love, the real interior and social condition of the people around you, to detect their true aspirations, foresee their difficulties, help them in their needs, be to them brothers in sincere service of their dignity, and collaborators in their destiny of freedom and their personal vocation for the Absolute. Walk together in carrying out such a high task, which demands a joint effort, mutual support, reciprocal aid, in order to defeat and overcome the recurrent temptations of discouragement, loss of confidence and selfish isolation.

I exhort you, then, to look to and follow Jesus Christ, the Revealer of the Father's love and the Constructor of man's true destiny, which goes beyond the limits of time and the barriers of history, and in His victory over evil and death you will find the most solid guarantee of your victory.

With these wishes, I impart to you and to all the members of your association my affectionate blessing.

Full Responsibility and Commitment

On April 30, 1980, the Holy Father addressed a paternal greeting to the young.

A fatherly greeting now goes to you young people, present at this audience, and always so dear to me because, with your world full of life and enthusiasm, you mean such hope for the Church of God.

"Young people"—the Council says—"exert a very important influence in modern society" (A.A. no. 12). Be aware of this great reality, showing in the first place full responsibility and commitment in carrying out your duties and generous enthusiasm in the accomplishment of the specific mission of each one of you.

May you be assisted in this program of life by the Virgin Mary, who offers you, in the coming month of May dedicated to her, the example of her virtues, while I willingly bless you.

What a Wonderful Thing!

The following is Pope John Paul II's message to the young people of Australia during National Vocations Awareness Week in April, 1980.

To all the young people of Australia I now repeat what I have told young people elsewhere: "Heed the call of Christ when you hear Him saying to you: 'Follow me!' Walk in my path! Stand by my side! Remain in my love!" Do not be afraid. It is a wonderful thing to be able to communicate Christ's peace, to promote His justice, to spread His truth, to proclaim and to live His love.

And if Christ is truly calling you to the priesthood or to the religious life, do not be afraid to say *yes*. Do not be afraid of a unique and permanent commitment to Christ. Do not hesitate to rely on His strength, to believe that His love will sustain you forever in the service of your brothers and sisters.

Remember that the power of Christ's Paschal Mystery will supply for your weakness and fill your hearts with love. And the Mother of Jesus will never abandon you.

Dear young people: this is a special hour for you and for the whole Christian community. It is an hour of commitment and responsibility, an hour of generosity and joy! Will you not open wide your hearts to Christ's call and to mine: Come, follow me!

And may the entire Church in Australia be filled with a renewed sense of mission and with fresh vigor and strength: in the name of the Father, and of the Son, and of the Holy Spirit. Amen.

To Be Like Jesus the Priest

On the afternoon of May 9, 1980, the Holy Father delivered the following address to 150 seminarians assembled in the seminary garden at Kumasi, Ghana. Later he went to Kumasi Airport and returned to Accra by plane.

Dear seminarians,

I am always happy to talk to young men who are preparing for the priesthood. Today I am particularly happy to meet you in your own country.

Even though you are young, you are able by your lives to teach the world a great lesson. What is this lesson? It is the lesson of *faith*. Your lives show that you believe in Jesus Christ and that you want to follow Him. You accept Him as God, as the Son of God who took on a human nature, who became man, and who became your brother and mine. You believe that He died on the cross and became your Savior and mine. And you believe that He rose from the dead and made it possible for you and me and everybody to live forever. This is the Jesus whom you have come to know and love, the Jesus in whom you have put your faith.

Yes, you believe in the Person of Jesus, and you also believe that His grace is strong—that it can overcome sin. You believe that Jesus can give you the grace to follow Him, to come after Him, to be like Him. *And that is what you want to do: to be like Jesus the Priest*—to spread the

Good News that Jesus brought, to tell the world about salvation, and to give people the bread of eternal life.

So faith in Jesus is important for you now and in the future. *Your life as a seminarian depends on faith;* faith is the foundation of the life of every priest. Faith means accepting Jesus into your lives, taking His message into your hearts, obeying His commandments. It also means being filled with the joy and love of Jesus. And the more this happens, the more you will be able to show Jesus to the world—the Jesus who lives in you and who wants to work through you.

When you live by faith and follow Christ's commandments, *you are able to give a dynamic example to other young people.* You are able to show by your lives and by the example of your Christian joy that Jesus' love is important—important for you in your vocation, and important for all your brothers and sisters who are trying to discover the fullness of their humanity. Living in this way, you can see that you have already begun the task of communicating Christ, of bringing Him to your friends and to the other youth of Ghana.

At the same time your fidelity to Christ, your courage to say *yes* to your special vocation, your faith in the power of Jesus to sustain you in His love during your whole life is a strong support for other young people of your age who have heard the call of the Good Shepherd and want to follow it faithfully. You know how much your country and all Africa needs priests—workers in the Lord's harvest. Remember the words of Jesus: "...lift up your eyes, and see how the fields are white for the harvest" (Jn. 4:35). *And pray for vocations,* pray for perseverance in your own vocation, pray that the Church in Africa will have the strength and fervor to supply the priests that Christ needs to preach His Gospel and to carry His message of salvation throughout this continent.

Dear seminarians: stay close to Jesus through prayer and the Holy Eucharist. And so by the way you live, let everybody know that you really do have faith, that you really believe in our Lord Jesus Christ.

And stay close also to our Blessed Mother Mary and to her Immaculate Heart. When Mary said *yes* to the angel, the mystery of redemption took shape beneath her heart. This pure heart of Mary was the inspiration for many of the missionaries who brought the Word of God to the African people. And for the Church today this heart of Mary continues to express the mystery of the Mother in redemption (cf. *Redemptor hominis,* no. 22).

In the name of Jesus, I bless you all. And I commend you and your families and friends to Mary, who is the Mother of us all.

"You Can Move Mountains"

In the afternoon of May 11, 1980, John Paul II traveled by helicopter from Abidjan to Yamoussoukro, Ivory Coast. On his arrival there he concelebrated Mass with thirteen young priests for the student youth of the country. The celebration was held in the largest square of Yamoussoukro, which by presidential decree of May 10 is now known as John Paul II Square. It was estimated that more than 200,000 were present. During the Mass, the Holy Father preached the following homily.

Dear students, boys and girls,

How can I thank you for having come in such large numbers, so joyful and trusting around the Father and Head of the Catholic Church? I hope and I ask God that this meeting may be a moment of deep communion of our hearts and minds, an unforgettable moment for me and a decisive one for you.

Your problems and aspirations as Ivory Coast students have come to my knowledge. They make me both happy and moved. It is, therefore, young people, in a concrete setting and bearers of great human and Christian hopes, that I address with perfect confidence. The Liturgy of the Word, which has just ended, has certainly contributed to putting your souls in a state of receptiveness. These three readings constitute an ideal framework for the demanding meditation we shall make shortly.

The Church, of which you are members through the sacraments of Baptism and Confirmation—I shall have,

moreover, the joy of conferring the latter on some of you—
is a Church that has been open, since her foundation, to all
men and all cultures; a Church assured of a glorious conclusion through the humiliations and persecutions inflicted
upon her in the course of history; a Church mysteriously
animated by the Spirit of Pentecost and eager to reveal to
men their inalienable dignity and their vocation as "members of God's family," creatures inhabited by God, Father,
Son and Spirit. How bracing it is to breathe this atmosphere
of a Church always young and resolute!

Your bishops have recently addressed to you, but also
to your parents and those in charge of you, a letter intended to diagnose the dangers that threaten youth and
bring about, in its ranks as well as among adults, a generous
spiritual outburst. Many of you are very conscious of the
difficulties and miseries affecting the environments of the
young. Without generalizing, they are not afraid to call a
spade a spade and to question their elders, referring to the
famous words of the prophet Ezekiel: "The fathers have
eaten sour grapes, and the children's teeth are set on edge
(Ez. 18:2).

A Call to Personal Conversion

Today, on my part, I would like to convince you of a
truth of common sense but of fundamental importance,
which applies to every man and every society that is suffering physically or morally: namely, that a sick person cannot
get better unless he himself takes the necessary remedies.
That is what the apostle St. James wished to make the first
Christians understand (cf. Jas. 1:23-26). What is the use of
diagnosing the disease in the mirror of individual and collective conscience, if we forget it immediately or refuse to
treat it? Everyone in society bears responsibilities with

regard to this situation and each one is called, therefore, to a personal conversion which is truly a form of participation in the evangelization of the world (cf. *Evangelii nuntiandi*, nos. 21, 41). But I ask you: is it not true that if all the young agree to change their own lives, the whole of society will change? Why wait longer for ready-made solutions to the problems from which you are suffering? Your dynamism, your imagination, your faith are capable of moving mountains!

Let us look together, calmly and realistically at the ways that will lead you towards the society of which you are dreaming. A society built on truth, justice, brotherhood, peace; a society worthy of man and in conformity with God's plan. These ways are inescapably those of your ardent preparation for your responsibilities tomorrow and those of a true spiritual awakening.

Young people of the Ivory Coast, find again together the courage to live! The men who cause history to advance, at the humblest or at the highest level, are those who remain convinced of man's vocation: the vocation of a searcher, of one who strives vigorously, and of a builder. What is your conception of man? It is a fundamental question, because the answer will determine your future and the future of your country, because it is your duty to make a success of your lives.

You Are a Privileged Youth

You have, indeed, obligations towards the national community. The past generations carry you invisibly. It is they who enabled you to have access to studies and a culture destined to make you the executives of a young nation. The people count on you. Forgive it for considering you privileged persons. You really are privileged, at least on the plane of the distribution of cultural goods. How many young people of your age—in your country and in the world—are at work and are contributing already, as workers or farmers, to the production and economic success of their country! Others, alas, are unemployed, without a trade, and sometimes without hope. Others again have not and will not have the chance to have access to schooling of quality. You have a duty of solidarity towards all. And they have the right to be demanding with regard to you. Dear young people, do you want to be the thinkers, the technicians, the leaders that your country and Africa need? Avoid like the plague carelessness and the easy way out. Be indulgent to others and severe with regard to yourselves! Be men!

Preserve Roots and Safeguard Values

Allow me, further, to stress a very important aspect of your human, intellectual and technical preparation for your future tasks. It is also part of your duties. Preserve carefully your African roots. Safeguard the values of your culture. You know them and are proud of them: respect for life, family solidarity and support for relatives, respect for the old, the sense of hospitality, judicious preservation of traditions, the taste for feasts and symbols, attachment to dialogue and palaver to settle differences. All that is a real treasure from which you can and must draw something new for the building up of your country, on an original and typically African model, made up of harmony between the values of its cultural past and the most acceptable elements of modern civilization. On this precise plane, remain very vigilant, with regard to models of society which are based on the selfish pursuit of individual happiness and on the god of money, or on the class struggle and violent means. All materialism is a source of degradation for man and of enslavement of social life.

Look with New Eyes Towards Jesus

Let us go even further in clear vision of the road to take or to continue. Who is your God? Without ignoring any of the difficulties that the social and cultural changes of our time cause all believers, but also thinking of all those who struggle to keep the faith, I venture to say concisely and insistently: Look up! Look with new eyes towards Jesus Christ! I take the liberty of asking you in a friendly way: have you read the letter I wrote last year to all Christians about Christ the Redeemer? In the wake of the Popes who preceded me, Paul VI especially, I endeavored to ward off the temptation and error of modern man and modern societies to exclude God and to put an end to the expression of the religious sentiment.

The death of God in men's hearts and lives is the death of man. I wrote in that letter: "The man who wishes to understand himself thoroughly—and not just in accordance with immediate, partial, often superficial, and even illusory standards and measures of his being—must with his unrest, uncertainty and even his weakness and sinfulness, with his life and death, draw near to Christ. He must, so to speak, enter into Him with all his own self, he must "appropriate" and assimilate the whole of the reality of the Incarnation and redemption in order to find himself. If this profound process takes place within him, he then bears fruit not only of adoration of God but also of deep wonder at himself. How precious must man be in the eyes of the Creator, if he 'gained so great a Redeemer,' and if God 'gave his only Son'

in order that man 'should not perish but have eternal life!' "
(*Redemptor hominis,* no. 10) Yes, beloved young people,
Jesus Christ is not a kidnapper of men, but a Savior. And He
wants to free you, to make you, one and all, saviors in the
student world of today as in the professions and important
responsibilities that you will assume tomorrow.

Faith Is Truly a Gift from God

So stop thinking to yourself or saying out loud that the
Christian faith is good only for children and simple people.
If it still appears to be so, it is because adolescents and
adults have seriously neglected to make their faith grow at
the same rate as their human development. Faith is not a
pretty garment for childhood days. Faith is a gift from God,
a stream of light and power that comes from Him, and must
enlighten and give dynamic impulse to all sectors of life, in
proportion as it takes root in responsibilities. Make up your
minds, and persuade your friends and fellow students, to
adopt the means of a personal religious formation, worthy
of the name. Take advantage of the chaplains and anima-
tors placed at your disposal. With them, train yourselves to
make a synthesis between your human knowledge and
your faith, between your African culture and modernity,
between your role as citizens and your Christian vocation.
Celebrate your faith and learn to pray together.

You will find again in this way the sense of the Church
which is communion in the same Lord among believers,
who then go out into the midst of their brothers and sisters
to love them and serve them in the way of Christ. You have
a vital need of integration in Christian, brotherly and
dynamic communities. Frequent them assiduously. Inspire
them with the breath of your youth. Build them if they do
not exist. In this way your temptation to go and seek

elsewhere—in esoteric groups—what Christianity brings you fully, will disappear.

Apostolic Commitment

Logically, the personal and community deepening of faith of which we have just spoken must lead you to concrete apostolic commitments. Many of you are already on this way, and I congratulate you. Young people of the Ivory Coast, today Christ calls you through His representative on earth. He calls you exactly as He called Peter and Andrew, James and John, and the other Apostles. He calls you to construct His Church, to build a new society. Come in crowds! Take your place in your Christian communities. Offer royally your time and your talents, your heart and your faith to animate liturgical celebrations, to take part in the immense amount of catechetical work among children, adolescents and even adults, and to be integrated in the numerous services for the benefit of the poorest, illiterates, the handicapped, the isolated, refugees and migrants, to animate your student movements, to work with the authorities for the defense and promotion of the human person. Truly, the workyard is immense and stirring for young people who feel overflowing with life.

It seems to me the very moment to address those young people who are going to receive the sacrament of Confirmation, precisely in order to enter a new stage of their baptismal life: the stage of active service in the immense workyard of the evangelization of the world. The laying on of hands and the anointing with the holy chrism will really and effectively signify the plenary coming of the Holy Spirit into the very depth of your person, at the crossroads, in a way, of your human faculties of intelligence in search of truth and freedom, in pursuit of an ideal. Your

Confirmation today is your Pentecost for life! Realize the seriousness and grandeur of this sacrament.

What will be your lifestyle from now on? That of the Apostles when they came out of the Upper Room! That of Christians of every era, energetically faithful to prayer, to deepening of, and bearing witness to, faith, to the breaking of the Eucharistic Bread, to service of one's neighbor and especially of the poorest (cf. Acts 2:42-47). Young confirmed persons of today or yesterday, advance all of you along the ways of life as fervent witnesses of Pentecost, an inexhaustible source of youth and dynamism for the Church and for the world.

Expect to meet sometimes with opposition, contempt, mockery. True disciples are not above the Master. Their crosses are like the passion and cross of Christ: a mysterious source of fruitfulness. This paradox of suffering offered and fruitful has been confirmed for twenty centuries by the history of the Church.

Allow me finally to assure you that such apostolic commitments prepare you not only to bear your heavy responsibilities in the future, but also to found solid homes, without which a nation cannot hold out long; and what is more, Christian homes, which are so many basic cells of the ecclesial community. There are commitments which will lead some of you towards complete donation to Christ, in the priesthood or religious life. The dioceses of the Ivory Coast, like all the dioceses of Africa, have the right to rely on your generous response to the call that the Lord certainly makes many of you hear: "Come and follow me."

A flash in the pan, this celebration? A flash in the pan, this meditation? The liturgical texts of this sixth Sunday of Easter affirm the contrary. The Gospel of John assures us that the Holy Spirit dwells in the loving and faithful hearts of the disciples of Christ. His role is to refresh their memory as believers, to enlighten them in depth, to help them to solve the problems of their time, in the peace and hope of the new world conjured up in the reading from Revelation.

May this same Holy Spirit unite us all and dedicate us all to the service of God our Father and of men our brothers, through Christ, in Christ, and with Christ! Amen.

Be Worthy

During the general audience of May 14, 1980, Pope John Paul II exhorted the young in the following words.

I greet the young present here and assure them of my most sincere esteem. I want to say only one thing to you: always be worthy of the expectations and the hopes that society and the Church place in you. Commit yourselves generously never to disappoint what the future of the world, as far as it lies in your hands, expects from your contribution of intelligence and love. It is these resolutions of yours and your efforts in this direction that I bless with all my heart.

If You Look to the Future You Will Make History

On May 18, 1980, the Holy Father celebrated in front of the Vatican Basilica the Mass for the Focolarini, *at the conclusion of the* GEN Fest 1980, *at which young people from 58 countries were present.*

John Paul II delivered the following homily.

Beloved young people of the GEN Movement!

I bid you all a hearty welcome. The joy that shines on your faces and is expressed in your songs has created around this Eucharistic Celebration an atmosphere of intimate and deep communion, the characteristic of a family, gathered around the hearth *(focolare)*.

Yes, the "hearth": a term which has a deep meaning for you. One thinks spontaneously of that first "hearth," constituted by the disciples gathered in the Upper Room (cf. Acts 1:13), after the Ascension of the Lord. The book of the Acts describes them as "with one accord (they) devoted themselves to prayer, together with...Mary" (cf. *ibid.*, v. 14), waiting for the coming of the Holy Spirit, whom they had been promised by the Master. In that expectation, in that prayer, in that brotherly union which they form—preparing for the first Coming and then, through that same Coming, living in charity—there is realized in its deepest principle that motto, "for a united world," which is the demanding motto of this meeting of yours. From this fusion, which took place in the Upper Room, the whole spirituality of the *Focolarini* finds, it could be said, its beginning and its source.

The movement, of which you are an expression, has its focal center in love, which the Spirit of Christ spreads in the hearts of believers. The world today is in immense need of this love. You are fully aware of it: You have reflected at length on the tensions which set against one another individuals, social classes, economic and political areas, groups inspired by different ideologies and faiths. In particular, you have realized the divisions and contradictions introduced among mankind by those ideologies which have a common materialistic basis and which, if closely examined, are seen to have no other ultimate prospect but the dreadful one of mutual destruction.

But you, beloved young people, have not resigned yourselves before these realities. With the enthusiasm that is typical of your age, you have not yielded to the present, you have turned your gaze to the future, in the confident hope of being able to leave to those who come after you a better world than the one you found.

What inspires such confidence in you? Whence do you draw the courage to plan and attempt the tremendous undertaking of the construction of a united world? It seems to me that I can hear the answer that bursts from your hearts: "In the word of Jesus. It was He who asked us to love one another to the point of becoming one thing. In fact, He prayed for this."

It is so, indeed: We have listened to His words in the passage of the Gospel just proclaimed. Jesus spoke those words at the Last Supper, a few hours before beginning His passion. They are words in which the supreme anxiety of the heart of the Word Incarnate is contained. Jesus presents this anxiety to the Father as to Him who alone can understand all its intensity and urgency and who alone is able to respond to it effectively. Jesus asks of the Father the gift of unity among all those who will believe in Him: "That they may all be one."

It is not a question of a recommendation addressed directly to us. It is worth stressing this. Jesus, who knows us thoroughly (cf. Jn. 2:24f.), knows that He cannot rely particularly on us for the implementation of such a radical project. An intervention from on high is necessary, which, elevating our petty hearts in the current of love that flows between the divine Persons, makes us capable of overcoming the barriers of selfishness and of opening ourselves to the "you" of brothers in a vital communion, in which each one will lose himself as an individual to find himself again in a "we," which speaks with the very voice of Christ, the first-born of the new humanity.

The Second Vatican Council referred to this when, with regard to the same passage of Scripture, it spoke of "new horizons closed to human reason," vistas from which it appears, however, that man, the only creature on earth that God wanted for its own sake "can fully discover his true self only in a sincere giving of himself" (Const. *Gaudium et spes,* no. 24).

We can catch a glimpse of these "closed vistas," and venture into them, if we open ourselves to the grace of Christ, who raises us to participation itself in the life of the Trinity. The lofty mystery of the eternal communion between the Father, the Son and the Holy Spirit then becomes the exemplary model and, as it were, the source that nourishes the communion that must be established among men: "Even as you, Father, are in me, and I in you, that they also may be in us" (Jn. 17:21).

"In us": Full unity cannot be constructed on any other foundation. It is necessary, therefore, for everyone to commit himself, in the first place, to the pursuit of an ever deeper union with God, by means of faith, the dialogue of prayer, and purification of the heart, if he wants to contribute effectively to the construction of unity. For the believer, the vertical dimension of openness to God and the relationship with Him is the premise that conditions all other commitments in the horizontal dimension of relationships with brothers.

This, however, does not mean, as is obvious, that the effort aimed at establishing new relationships of sincere cordiality with brothers is unimportant. The quality of these relationships is, indeed, according to the teaching of Scripture, a criterion to check the authenticity of the relationship which one claims to have with God (cf. 1 Jn. 4:20; 3:17). The effort to construct unity appears in this way as the test by which every Christian must verify the seriousness of his own adherence to the Gospel.

What will be, in practice, the attitude of the Christian in preparing to meet his fellow men? It will have to be fundamentally an attitude of confidence and esteem. The Christian must believe in man, believe in "all his capacity for greatness but at the same time with his need to be redeemed from the evil and sin within him" (cf. no. 2).

I said this in the message at the beginning of the year for the World Day of Peace (cf. no. 2); and I am happy to repeat, on this particularly significant occasion, the urgency of delving deep down in ourselves in order to reach those areas in which—beyond the divisions that we see in ourselves and between ourselves—we can discover that the specific dynamisms of man lead him to meeting, to mutual respect, brotherhood and peace (cf. *ibid.*, no. 4).

When we look at things in this perspective, we are spontaneously led to understand the other person and his reasons, to reduce any errors of his to their real proportions, to correct or integrate our own point of view on the basis of the new aspects of truth that have emerged from the comparison. In particular, we are able to avoid the attitude of those who, in the heat of polemics, end up by discrediting those who think differently, attributing to them dishonest intentions and wrong methods (cf. *ibid.*, no. 5).

Only he who cultivates sincere respect for his fellow man can open a fruitful and constructive dialogue with him. In that message I defined dialogue as "an indispensable means for attaining peace" *(ibid.*, no. 8). It is so, indeed, at least when the one who practices it endeavors to abide by the rules that govern it. My Predecessor, Pope Paul VI, described it admirably in his Encyclical *Ecclesiam suam:* "The dialogue," he recalled, "is not proud, it is not cutting, it is not offensive. Its authority is intrinsic because of the truth it sets forth, the charity it spreads, the example it proposes; it is not a command, it is not an imposition. It is peaceful; it avoids violent ways; it is patient; it is generous" (no. 83).

Dialogue: that is the way along which it is possible to take great strides towards an ever deeper agreement and towards that unity which is always a perfectible aim here below, because it is never entirely achieved.

There is, however, a prerequisite that conditions any serious effort in this direction: it consists in the readiness to forgive.

Sin is part of the bag and baggage of historical man. It is not possible, therefore, to imagine that one can meet man without meeting sin. A realistic approach to dialogue cannot but take into consideration also the necessity of "reconciliation" between persons divided by sin. For this reason Jesus emphasized so forcefully the duty of forgiveness, to the extent of making it the condition for being able to hope, in turn, for God's forgiveness (cf. Mt. 6:12, 14-15; 18:35).

He, in person, gave us the example, because on the cross absolute innocence and the sheerest wickedness met. The prayer: "Father, forgive them for they know not what they do" (Lk. 23:34) deprives us of any possible pretext of withdrawing into ourselves and refusing forgiveness.

St. Stephen had understood this perfectly. In the First Reading of this liturgy we saw him, falling beneath the blows of the stones, and uttering the words that make his moral greatness stand out forever: "Lord, do not hold this sin against them" (Acts 7:60).

Beloved young people, the new generation that bears the world of the future in its hands! You have decided to make love the inspiring norm of your lives. For this reason the commitment for unity has become your program. It is an eminently Christian program. The Pope is, therefore, very happy to encourage you to continue along this way, whatever it may cost. You must give your contemporaries the testimony of generous enthusiasm and inflexible constancy in the commitment required by the determination to construct a united world.

You know where to find the source from which to draw the energies necessary for this difficult path: It lies in the heart of Him who is "the Alpha and the Omega, the first and the last, the beginning and the end" (Rv. 22:13). It is said of Him that He offers everyone "the water of life without price" *(ibid.,* v. 17).

Let Christ be everywhere your sure point of reference; He is the foundation of a trust that never wavers. Let the passionate invocation of the Church: "Come, Lord Jesus," become the spontaneous yearning of your heart, never satisfied with the present, because it is always straining towards the "not yet" of the promised fulfillment.

Beloved young people, your lives must carry out to the world your faith in Him who said: "Behold, I am coming soon, bringing my recompense" (Rv. 22:12). You must be the vanguard of the people walking towards those "new heavens" and that "new earth in which righteousness dwells" (2 Pt. 3:13). The men who are able to look to the future are those who make history; the others are carried along by it and end up excluded, caught up in a network of occupations, plans and hopes which, in the end, are seen to be fallacious and alienating. Only those who commit themselves in the present, without letting themselves be "captured" by it, but remaining with the eyes of the heart fixed on "the things that are above, where Christ is, seated at the right hand of God" (Col. 3:1), can direct history towards its fulfillment.

This Eucharistic celebration of ours is an anticipation "in mystery" of this fulfillment. Now, as at every Mass, the invocation of the Church, the bride of Christ still subjected to the tribulations of the present world, is joined by that of the Spirit: "The Spirit and the Bride say, 'Come'" (Rv. 22:17). The liturgy of the earth is harmonized with that of heaven. Now, as at every Mass, our heart, in need of comfort, receives the reassuring answer: "He who testifies to these things says, 'Surely I am coming soon'" *(ibid.,* v. 20).

Sustained by this certainty, we continue again on our way along the paths of the world, feeling more united and in solidarity with one another and, at the same time, bearing in our hearts a more ardent desire to bring to brothers, still wrapped in the shadows of doubt and discouragement, the "good news" that "the bright morning star," the Redeemer of man, Christ the Lord, has risen also on the horizon of their existence (Rv. 22:1).

A Day of Rejoicing Concluded with Song

May 18, 1980, was Pope John Paul II's 60th birthday. At 9:00 p.m., when he returned from visiting the Roman parish of Christ the King, he found the Courtyard of St. Damasus illuminated and extraordinarily alive with singing and the enthusiasm of about three thousand young people sitting on the cobblestones waiting patiently for his arrival. The young people sang for a long time, offering a wide repertory of folkloristic songs from the various regions of Italy, with Polish songs interspersed. Then some young people performed an Italian popular dance.

After ending their songs and dances in honor of the Pope, they asked him to speak. The Holy Father, visibly happy at being among the young, addressed them briefly as follows.

It is clear that young people rejoice when an old man becomes older: but I said this morning that, becoming older, I must also become younger, and I have repeated this to myself all day long. I thank you heartily for this meeting, always very interesting for me. I would also like this meeting to last until tomorrow morning, but there is a rhythm of work that creates obstacles. For me it is always interesting to participate in what Communion and Liberation means, how Communion and Liberation lives, and how communion and liberation is lived. Certainly it is lived with one another, through an experience of song that creates communion; I have known this experience for so many years and I see that you, too, have a perfect knowledge of it: Communion is lived through song. A deep study should be made of how song creates communion. I am not so surprised when it is said that in heaven the angels sing. Perhaps they do not sing songs from Abruzzo but something similar which shows the intensity and depth, the spontaneity and directness of communion among persons. I thank you for this brief, but for me so precious, experience of communion through song and also through dancing.

We must conclude this meeting, which is not yet the last of the day. I would like to invite you for another meeting of song and dancing. We shall arrange the day, or rather the evening, and we shall also arrange the place. I hope that we shall be able to continue with this experience of Communion and Liberation, because liberation is a fruit of communion. Man is structured in this way. God created man's personal nature in such a way that it lives in communion and is liberated in communion: man cannot liberate himself otherwise, alone. To liberate oneself means arriving at fulfillment through the gift of oneself, which is always the foundation of communion. I want to thank you for the short time in which we have been able to live communion through the gifts offered by all those present.

I have seen that you have a heart capable of sympathy. Thanking you, I want to invite you again to return. For me these evenings of ours are very agreeable and instructive. Now let us recite the *Our Father* for all the young people of your community and for all the young people of Italy and the world.

The Sign
of the Holy Spirit

During the general audience of May 21, 1980, Pope John Paul II reminded the young people present of the importance of the coming feast of Pentecost.

I now extend my cordial greeting to all boys and girls and young people gathered here to express to the Pope their sentiments of deep faith and affectionate devotion.

Beloved in Christ, bidding you a cordial welcome, I am glad to remind you of the imminence of the feast of Pentecost, which is an event of fundamental importance for the Church: her presentation to the world, the official birth with baptism in the Spirit! The fulfillment of Easter, the coming of the Holy Spirit on the disciples of the risen Christ—of yesterday, today and of all times—is a principle of new life, the life of truth, grace and love for their hearts and their activity. The whole life of the Christian is, therefore, under the sign and influence of the Holy Spirit, received in Baptism and in Confirmation which are "our Pentecost." While I address a special thought to all those who have received First Communion or the sacrament of Confirmation in these days, I willingly bless you.

In Your Studies
Look for Christ

On May 23, 1980, the Holy Father received in audience the young pupils of St. Alexander's Episcopal School of Bergamo accompanied by the rector and the teaching staff. The group was led by Bishop Giulio Oggioni of Bergamo and was composed of about 600 persons, including also the parents of the pupils.

The Holy Father delivered the following address.

Dear boys of St. Alexander's Episcopal School!

I thank you sincerely for this visit, which offers me the opportunity to see you gathered here and to address to you my affectionate word of exhortation. In particular I thank your zealous Bishop, Most Reverend Giulio Oggioni, for the noble and meaningful words which, interpreting also your sentiments, he has kindly addressed to me. My cordial greeting is extended to your parents, to the whole teaching staff and, above all, to your rector, Don Achille Sana, for the initiative of this Roman pilgrimage to St. Peter's tomb and to the dwelling of his Successor in the See of Rome.

Your presence awakens in my heart the esteem I cherish for Bergamo, the beautiful Lombard city from which you come. It evokes its ancient and recent history, its old Christian traditions, its cultural institutions—including your school, which boasts over a century of life and activity—its strong people, hard-working and generous; but above all it recalls to my mind and my heart the dear and fatherly figure of your greatest fellow countryman and my venerated Predecessor, Pope John XXIII. He left a deep mark on the life of the Church of our century and filled the whole world with his memory, illustrating and thus glorifying his native land and the genius of his people, as well as the Roman Pontificate.

Dear boys, as the direct heirs of such a rich religious tradition, be conscious and deserving of belonging to St. Alexander's Episcopal School, from which there have come forth illustrious men, who have played such a part in your culture. Appreciate the fortune that is granted to you of belonging to it and consider what an opportunity it offers you to be initiated into the noble and authentic experiences of intellectual and moral life. Keep your eyes open and your hearts ready to respond to the requirements and expectations of your superiors, your families and modern society with an earnest, serene and constructive commitment in the academic and disciplinary field.

I would like so much to become acquainted with each of you, and know what your studies are, and what is the cultural climate of your school and the spiritual atmosphere of your school community. I like to think of it—and I hope it may be such—as a mutual understanding of hearts, made up of fruitful collaboration between superiors and pupils, between teachers and students; well ordered for intensity of studies and resolutions, for awareness of what you are and of what you want to become.

But above all I say to you: Be young people who are able to look for Christ, know Him and love Him. Have faith in Him: be *"fortes in fide,"* as the Apostle Peter exhorted in his first letter (5:9). The Church wants a strong faith from you, and the commitment of your will demands it. Have the courage to exercise it, breathe it and profess it not only interiorly to experience its light and sweetness, but also exteriorly to express it in words, in song and in daily conduct.

St. Peter from his nearby tomb recommends and repeats to you today, here in Rome, in the center of Christendom, the sublime and salutary lesson of how to believe, how to overcome weaknesses and obstacles, and how to be really Christians.

In this way, boys, you will be able to sanctify also your study and make it your great love, and you will find the strength to overcome conventional laziness and hypocrisy; you will have the capacity and the pleasure of rising to the understanding of others and to meet the problems of our time in an attitude of friendship, industry and service. You will be able to live in your school with your hearts full of pure and good joy, and you will be able to do a great deal of good to the young people around you. I hope that in this way you will be able to bring to your institute further credit and offer society a precious contribution of moral, as well as cultural, well-being, and profess to Christ a testimony of incomparable value, deserving to be called and to be really true sons of the Church, strong, faithful and generous.

With these thoughts and with these wishes I invoke on each of you the protection of the Blessed Virgin, the Seat of Wisdom, and of St. Alexander, your heavenly patron, while I willingly impart to you the propitiating apostolic blessing.

Everyone Anxiously Awaits You!

On the afternoon of May 24, 1980, the Holy Father visited the Roman Minor Seminary and delivered the following address to the pupils in the seminary chapel.

Beloved brothers and sons,

How can I tell you my great joy at finding myself in your midst today? This is a visit that I have owed you for some time. Certainly, of all those carried out in various parts of the diocese of Rome, this is among the most desired and significant. Indeed, it offers me the possibility of meeting personally the members and leaders of the community which cultivates, as in a seedbed, those shoots destined to become the ministers indispensable for the Christian life of this local Church, which is the diocese of the Pope. Therefore, it is with special warmth that I greet you all, seminarians both day-boys and boarders, and teachers of the Roman Minor Seminary, for whom my most genuine fatherly affection is reserved.

Today's meeting gives me the opportunity to address, in the first place, a special word of encouragement to the adolescents of the seminarian boarding school community. To them I say to proceed always quickly and joyfully towards the goal of the priesthood. There you are already anxiously awaited: by the Lord, to whom you conform yourselves in a very special way; by the bishop, with whom you are called to share pastoral responsibilities; and by the whole Christian community, on behalf of which you spend your lives to help it to walk in growth of faith and of witness in the world.

Next, I wish to devote a special thought to the many boys and adolescents of the diocesan vocational community, which is, in a way, the "reserve" of the "team" more directly committed in consecration to Christ and to the Church. To them I say to remain always generously available to assume their role in the field, ready to place their energies and enthusiasm at the service of the Lord and the People of God, docilely accepting His invitation, when He says to you clearly: "Follow me!" Rest assured, in any case, that the Pope really expects a great deal from you too.

Besides that, I cannot pass over in silence the actual problem of vocations, the terms and urgency of which are before everyone's eyes. Loving and intelligent care of vocations is one of the prime necessities of the whole Church and must be a matter of great concern for the keener members of the diocesan community. I intend, therefore, to stimulate and encourage priests and sisters, already engaged in this difficult and precious apostolate in parishes and in Catholic schools, to intensify their efforts for an effective vocational catechesis. A special and important function in the apostolate of vocations belongs also to parents and families, which are often the starting point and favorable environment of maturation for a total dedication to the ministerial priesthood.

I assure all these categories of persons of my cordial esteem and my heartfelt thanks. Their lasting activity, together with the necessary grace of God, is the most concrete sign and the most reliable foundation of the hope and confidence that never abandons us, namely, that of seeing that the Lord does not fail "to send out laborers into his harvest" (Mt. 9:38).

My most spontaneous wish, therefore, is that all together you will continue joyfully and with abnegation along the path undertaken, well aware that the stake deserves every effort. May the Lord, to whom we must raise assiduous prayers, fecundate lavishly our resolutions, which are all directed to His greater glory and to the good of His holy Church.

The apostolic blessing, which I willingly impart to all of you present here and extend to your friends and collaborators as a sign of my benevolence and also of my serene confidence is a token of these wishes—which I entrust to the motherly intercession of the Blessed Virgin.

"The Necessity of the Lay Apostolate"

About 600 young people received the sacrament of Confirmation during the Holy Father's Mass in St. Peter's Basilica on Pentecost Sunday, May 25, 1980. The following is the text of the homily preached by His Holiness on the occasion.

Revered brothers and beloved sons!

Here there has come for us again, according to the order of the liturgical calendar, "the day of Pentecost"... (Acts 2:1), a day of special solemnity which takes its place, for its dignity of celebration and riches of spiritual content, alongside Easter Sunday itself. Is it possible to establish a comparison between the Pentecost of which the Acts of the Apostles speaks, that which took place fifty days after the resurrection of the Lord, and Pentecost today? Yes, this connection is not only possible, but certain, unquestioned and strengthening in the life and for the life of the Church, at the level both of her bimillenary history and of the present time in which we are living, as men of this generation. We have the right, the duty and the joy to say that Pentecost continues.

Rightly do we speak of the "perpetuity" of Pentecost. We know, in fact, that fifty days after Easter, the Apostles, gathered in that same Upper Room which had already been the place of the first Eucharist and, subsequently, of the first meeting with the risen Christ, discover in themselves the power of the Holy Spirit who had descended upon them, the power of Him whom the Lord had repeatedly promised them at the cost of His own suffering on the cross, and on the strength of this power, they begin to act, that is, to carry out their service. The apostolic Church is born. But today still—and here is the connection —St. Peter's Basilica, here in Rome, is, as it were, a prolongation, a continuation of the original Upper Room in Jerusalem, as is every church and chapel, as is every place in which the disciples and believers in the Lord are gathered: And we are assembled here to renew the mystery of this great day.

This mystery must be manifested particularly—as you know—by means of the sacrament of Confirmation, which the numerous Christian boys and girls of the diocese of Rome, who have come here, are about to receive today after due preparation. This morning my first greeting, to express the predilection and confidence I cherish for them, is addressed to these sons and daughters, precisely because they are to receive the "gift of the most High God" and to benefit from the ineffable action of His Spirit. My greeting is then extended to their godfathers, to their parents and relatives, and to all those who take part, in unity of intentions and sentiments, in this significant and inspiring celebration.

A Divine Gift
and Source of Sanctification

We must now reflect that Pentecost began precisely on the very evening of the resurrection, when the risen Lord—as the Gospel just proclaimed has told us (Jn. 20:19-20)—came for the first time among His Apostles in the Upper Room and, after greeting them by wishing them peace, He breathed on them and said: "Receive the Holy Spirit. If you forgive the sins of any, they are forgiven..." *(ibid.,* 22-23). This, then, is the paschal gift, because we are at the first day, that is, the generating element of that numerical series of days, in which the day of Pentecost is exactly the fiftieth, because we are at the starting point, which is the reality of the resurrection. Because of it, according to a relationship of causality prior even to a relationship of chronology, Christ gave the Holy Spirit to the Church as the divine gift and as the incessant and inexhaustible source of sanctification.

In other words, we must consider that, on the very evening of His resurrection, with a striking punctuality, Christ fulfills the promise made both in private and in public, to the woman of Samaria and to the crowd of the Jews, when He spoke of a living and health-giving water and invited the people to go to Him in order to be able to draw it abundantly and quench their thirst with it for ever (cf. Jn. 4:10, 13-14; 7:37). "Now he said this—the evangelist commented—about the Spirit, which those who believed in him were to receive; for as yet the Spirit had not been given, because Jesus was not yet glorified" (Jn. 7:39). So, as soon as He was glorified, that same promise of the sending-arrival *(quem mittet; cum venerit)* of the Paraclete Spirit, formally confirmed to His Apostles *"pridie quam pateretur"* (Jn. 14:16, 26; 15:26; 16:7-8, 13), is immediately satisfied.

"Receive the Holy Spirit...," and this gift of holiness at once begins to act: Sanctification starts—according to the very words of Jesus—with the remission of sins. First there is Baptism, the sacrament of the total cancellation of faults, whatever their number or their seriousness may be; then there is Penance, the sacrament of reconciliation with God and with the Church, and also the Anointing of the Sick.

But this work of sanctification always reaches its culminating point in the Eucharist, the sacrament of the fullness of holiness and grace: *Mens impletur gratia.*

In this admirable flow of supernatural life, what is the place of Confirmation? It must be said that sanctification itself is expressed also in strengthening, precisely in Confirmation. In it, too, indeed, there is the holy and sanctifying Spirit in superabundant fullness; in it there is the Spirit of Jesus to operate in a particular direction and with an efficacy quite its own: It is the dynamic direction, it is the efficacy of action inspired and directed from within. This, too, had been foreseen and predicted: "But stay in the city, until you are clothed with power from on high" (Lk. 24:49); "But you shall receive power when the Holy Spirit has come upon you" (Acts 1:8). The nature of the sacrament of Confirmation springs from this conferring of power which is communicated by the Spirit of God to each baptized person, to make him—according to the well-known catechetical terminology—a perfect Christian and a soldier of Christ, ready to bear witness with courage to His resurrection and redeeming virtue: "You shall be my witnesses" (Acts 1:8).

Growth in Community

If this is the particular meaning of Confirmation for the strengthening in us "of the inner man," in the triple line of faith, hope and charity, it is easy to understand how, as a direct consequence, it has a great significance also for the construction of the community of the Church, as the Body of Christ (cf. Second Reading from 1 Cor. 12). Due emphasis must be laid also on this second meaning, because it makes it possible to grasp, as well as the personal dimension, the community and, specifically, ecclesial dimension, in the strengthening action of the Spirit. We have listened to Paul

who spoke to us about this action and the distribution, by
the Spirit, of His charisms "for the common good." Is it not
true that in this exalted perspective there should be set the
vast subject of the apostolate and, especially, of the lay
apostolate, a subject which is of such topical interest? If "to
each is given the manifestation of the Spirit for the common good," how could a Christian feel extraneous or indifferent to, or exonerated from, the work of building the
Church?

The necessity of the lay apostolate is derived from this
and is defined as a due response to the gifts received. In this
connection, I think it will be well to take up again—I confine myself to a mere mention of it—that conciliar text
which, on the biblical and theological foundations of our
insertion through Baptism in the Mystical Body of Christ
and through the power received from the Spirit by means
of Confirmation, presents the ministry that appertains to
each member of the Church as a "noble obligation of working." "For the exercise of the apostolate—it is added—he
(the Holy Spirit) gives the faithful special gifts," from which
is derived correlatively the obligation of operating and
cooperating "for the building up of the whole body in
charity" (cf. Decree *Apostolicam Actuositatem*, introduc-
tion and no. 3).

An Indelible Mark

Confirmation—as we all know and as has been explained to you, dear boys and girls, upon whom it will be
conferred today—is received only once during life.
However, it must leave a lasting mark: Precisely because it
marks the soul indelibly, it can never be reduced to a distant memory or a fading religious practice, soon exhausted.
It is necessary, therefore, to ask ourselves how the

sacramental and vital meeting with the Holy Spirit, whom we have received from the hands of the Apostles by means of Confirmation, can and must last and become more deeply rooted in the lives of each of us. This is shown splendidly in the Pentecost Sequence *Veni Sancte Spiritus.* It reminds us, in the first place, that we must invoke with faith, with insistence, this admirable gift, and it teaches us also how we must invoke it. Come, O Holy Spirit, send us a ray of Your light.... Perfect Comforter, give us Your sweet relief, rest in fatigue and consolation in suffering. Give us Your power, because without it there is nothing in us, nothing is without sin!

As I mentioned at the beginning, Pentecost is a day of joy, and I would like to express, once more, this feeling, because in this way we can renew the mystery of Pentecost in St. Peter's Basilica. But the Spirit of God is not limited: It blows where it wills (Jn. 3:8), it penetrates everywhere, with sovereign and universal freedom. It is for this reason that from the interior of this basilica, as the humble Successor of that Peter who, precisely on the day of Pentecost, inaugurated the ministry of the Word with intrepidly apostolic courage, I now find the strength to cry *Urbi et Orbi:* "Come, Holy Spirit, fill the hearts of your faithful, and kindle within them the fire of your love." So may it be for the whole Church, for the whole of mankind!

"The Holy Spirit Illuminates Our Minds"

During the general audience on May 28, 1980, Pope John Paul II addressed the young people present urging them to invoke the Holy Spirit so as to better understand and hope in Jesus Christ.

To the young present at this audience, my cordial and affectionate greeting as usual.

Pentecost prompts us to address our prayer to the Holy Spirit. It is He who illuminates our minds to understand that Jesus Christ is man's secure hope, without which he lives in solitude and sadness.

May the Spirit of God, dear young people, fill also your hearts with His joy and renew your wills, making them docile to His inspirations.

Learn Jesus Christ: Place Yourself in His School

Before the Pope's journey to Paris on June 1, 1980, the youth of that city conducted a poll to draw up a list of questions to be submitted to the Pope in order that he might answer them in his address to them. The following is the full list of the twenty-one questions arrived at, and three of these were eventually chosen as the subject of the Holy Father's discourse in Parc des Princes.

Questions Addressed to the Pope by the Youth of Paris

1. In every country that you visited you wished to meet the youth. Why?

2. In each country you visited you wished to meet the rulers. Why? What did you say to them?

3. What do you expect to do for the unity of Christians? How do you see this unity?

4. How does one pray as Pope?

5. You have taken pretty severe measures in regard to some theologians. Why?

6. Two years have passed since your election: At this point, how do you see your ministry?

7. Tell us about your own country. What can we learn from Poland? And what can Poland learn from France?

8. You have been in Latin America and in Africa: How do you view the relations between the Third World and countries such as France?

9. Can the Gospel provide an answer for the problems of today?

10. Before being a bishop and Pope you were a simple priest. How do you view the priest of today?

11. People frequently speak of a Third World War. What can we young people do to prevent it?

12. We wish to be happy. Is it possible to be so in the present-day world?

13. Speak to us simply about Jesus Christ. Who is Jesus Christ for you?

14. Is it necessary to continue the work of Vatican II?

15. What can the Catholic Church do for peace and justice in the world?

16. The Catholic Church is ruled by men. Will women always have a secondary role?

17. As regards sexuality the Catholic Church always adopts decisions which are rather restrictive. Why? Do you not fear that the youth will gradually become estranged from the Church?

18. How can one be a witness of Christ today?

19. What is the role of the laity, and especially of the young, in the Church?

20. The Church is Western. Can it be really African or Asiatic?

21. If we had not submitted these questions to you, what would you have said to us?

The three questions addressed to the Pope in *Parc des Princes* were: If we had not submitted these questions to you, what would you have said to us?

Speak to us simply about Jesus Christ. Who is Jesus Christ for you?

People frequently speak of a Third World War. What can we young people do to prevent it?

In the course of his address, the Holy Father wished to give a complete reply to all twenty-one questions.

On the evening of Sunday, June 1, 1980, the Holy Father met over ninety thousand young Parisians gathered at Parc des Princes, *the largest stadium in the French capital, for a prayer vigil.*

The address that the Holy Father delivered to the young people during the meeting was not the one originally prepared for the occasion. The reason for this change was explained to the young people by the Pope himself who, before ending the meeting, said: "Before concluding I must tell you how I prepared this dialogue, this address-dialogue. I was sent the program and I was told that I had to speak to the young. So then I prepared a speech. Later the organizers sent me 'your' program and the questions you wished to ask the Pope. So it was necessary to change the address I had prepared and prepare the one you have just heard...."

Dear young people of France,

I thank you for this meeting which you wished to organize as a kind of dialogue. You wanted to speak to the Pope. And that is very important for two reasons.

The first reason is that this way of acting refers us directly to Christ: In Him, there is continually unfolded a dialogue: God's conversation with man and man's with God.

Christ—you have heard—is the Word, the Word of God. He is the eternal Word. This Word of God, like man, is not the word of a "great monologue," but the *Word* of the "incessant dialogue" which takes place in the Holy Spirit. I know that this sentence is difficult to understand, but I say it all the same, and I leave it to you so that you can meditate on it. Did we not celebrate this morning the mystery of the Holy Trinity?

The second reason is the following: the dialogue corresponds to my personal conviction that, to be the servant of the Word means "proclaiming" in the sense of "answering." To answer, it is necessary to know the questions. So it is a good thing that you asked them; otherwise, I would have had to guess in order to be able to speak to you, to answer you! (that is your question no. 21)

I have arrived at this conviction, not only because of my experience in the past as a teacher, through lectures or working groups, but above all through my experience as a preacher: giving the homily, and above all, preaching retreats. Most of the time I was addressing young people; they were young people that I was helping to meet the Lord, listen to Him, and also reply to Him.

Addressing you now, I would like to do so in such a way as to be able to *answer all your questions, at least indirectly.*

It is for this reason that I cannot do so taking them one after the other. In that case my answers would necessarily be only schematic!

So allow me to choose the question that seems to me the most important, the most central one, and to start with it. In this way, I hope that your other questions will appear gradually.

Your central question concerns Jesus Christ. You want to hear me speak of Jesus Christ, and you ask me who is Jesus Christ for me (it is your 13th question).

Allow me to return the question also and say to you Who is Jesus Christ for you? In this way, and without evading the question, I shall also give you my answer, telling you what He is for me.

The whole of the Gospel is a dialogue with man, with the different generations, with nations, with different traditions...; but it is always and continually a dialogue with man, with every man, one, unique, absolutely individual

At the same time, we find many dialogues in the Gospel. Among the latter, I choose as particularly eloquent, Christ's dialogue with the young man.

I will read you the text, because perhaps you do not remember it very well. It is in chapter 19 of the Gospel of Matthew.

"And behold, one came up to him, saying, 'Teacher, what good deed must I do to have eternal life?' And he said to him, 'Why do you ask me about what is good? One there is who is good. If you would enter life, keep the commandments.' He said to him, 'which?' And Jesus said, 'You shall not kill, You shall not commit adultery, You shall not steal, You shall not bear false witness, Honor your father and mother, and, You shall love your neighbor as yourself.' The young man said to him, 'All these I have observed; what do I still lack?' Jesus said to him, 'If you would be perfect, go, sell what you possess and give it to the poor, and you will have treasure in heaven; and come, follow me.' When the young man heard this he went away sorrowful; for he had great possessions."

Why does Christ dialogue with this young man? The answer is found in the Gospel narrative. And you, you ask me why, wherever I go, I want to meet the young (it is even your first question).

And I answer you: because "a young man" indicates a man who, in a special way, in a decisive way, is in the act of "forming himself." That does not mean that man does not form himself for the whole of his life: It is said that "education begins already before birth" and lasts to the last day. From the point of view of formation, however, youth is a particularly important, rich and decisive period. If you reflect on Christ's dialogue with the young man, you will find confirmation of what I have just said.

The young man's questions are essential ones. So are the answers.

These questions and these answers are not only essential for the young man concerned, important for his situation at that time; they are also of prime importance and essential for today. That is why, to the question whether the Gospel can answer the problems of modern men (it is your 9th question), I answer: Not only "is it capable of doing so," but we must go even further: It alone gives them a total answer, which goes to the bottom of things and completely.

I said at the beginning that Christ is the Word, the Word of an incessant dialogue. He is the *dialogue*, the dialogue with every man, although some people do not take part in it, not everyone knows how to—and there are also people who reject this dialogue explicitly. They move away.... And yet...perhaps this dialogue is in progress with them, too. I am convinced that this is so. More than once this dialogue "is revealed" in an unexpected and surprising way.

I note also your question why, in the various countries to which I go, and also in Rome, I speak to the various heads of State (question number 2).

Simply because Christ speaks to all men, to every man. Moreover, I think, rest assured, that there is no less to be said to men who have such great social responsibilities as to the young man of the Gospel, and to each of you.

To your question, what I speak about when I talk to heads of State, I will reply that I speak to them, very often, precisely of the young. In fact, "the day of tomorrow" depends on youth. These words are taken from a song that young Poles of your age often sing: "It is on us that the day of tomorrow depends." I, too, have sung it more than once with them. Furthermore, I generally enjoyed very much singing songs with the young, for the music and for the words. I recall this memory because you also asked me questions about my country (it is your 7th question), but to answer this question I should have to speak for a very long time!

And you also ask what France could learn from Poland, and what Poland could learn from France.

It is generally considered that Poland has learned more from France than the latter from Poland. Historically, Poland is several centuries younger. I think, however, that France could also learn various things. Poland has not had an easy history, especially in the course of the last few centuries. The Poles have "paid," and not just a little, in order to be Poles, and also to be Christians.... This answer is an "autobiographical" one, you will excuse me for this, but it was you who caused it. Allow me, however, to widen this autobiographical answer with the help of some other questions that you asked. For example, when you ask if the Church, which is "Western," can really be the "African" or "Asian" Church (20th question).

Of course, this question is much broader and goes further than the one about which I have just spoken with regard to the Church in France or in Poland. Both of them, in fact, are "Western," belonging to the field of the same European and Latin culture, but my answer will be the same. By her nature, the Church is one and universal. She becomes the Church of every nation, or of continents or races, in proportion as these societies accept the Gospel and make it, so to speak, their property. A short time ago, I went to Africa. Everything indicates that the young Churches of this continent are well aware of being African. And they are consciously aspiring to act as the link between Christianity and the traditions of their cultures. In Asia, and above all in the Far East, it is often thought that Christianity is the "Western" religion, and yet, I do not doubt that the Churches that have taken root there are "Asian" Churches.

Let us now return to our main subject, Christ's dialogue with the young man.

Actually, I would be inclined to say that we have remained all the time in its context.

The young man asks, then: "Teacher, what good deed must I do to have eternal life?" (Mt. 19:16)

Now you raise the question: Is it possible to be happy in the modern world? (it is your 12th question)....

As a matter of fact, you ask the same question as this young man!

Christ answers—to him and also to you, to each of you—it is possible. That is, in fact, what He answers, even if His words are the following: "If you would enter life, keep the commandments" (Mt. 19:17). And He will reply further later: "If you would be perfect, go, sell what you possess and give to the poor...and follow me" (cf. Mt. 19:21).

These words mean that man cannot be happy except to the extent to which he is capable of accepting the requirements that his own humanity, his dignity as a man, set him. The requirements that God sets him.

In this way, therefore, Christ does not only answer the question whether it is possible to be happy—but He says more: how we can be happy, on what condition. This answer is absolutely original, and it cannot be outdated, it can never be superseded. You must think about it carefully and adapt it to yourselves. Christ's answer consists of two parts. In the first one, it is a question of observing the commandments. Here, I will make a digression on account of one of your questions on the principles that the Church teaches in the field of sexual morality (the 17th question). You express your concern, seeing that they are difficult, and that young people might, precisely for this reason, turn away from the Church. I will answer you as follows. If you think deeply about this question, and if you go to the heart of the problem, I assure you that you will realize one thing: In this field, the Church sets only the requirements that are closely linked with true, that is responsible, married and conjugal love. She demands what the dignity of the person and fundamental social order requires. I do not deny that they are her demands. But the essential point of the problem lies precisely there: namely, that man fulfills himself only to the extent to which he is able to impose demands on himself. Otherwise, he goes away "sorrowful," as we have just read in the Gospel. Moral permissiveness does not make men happy. The consumer society does not make men happy. They have never done so.

In Christ's dialogue with the young man, there are, as I said, two stages. In the first one, it is a question of the ten commandments, that is, the fundamental requirements of all human morality. In the second stage, Christ says: "If you would be perfect...come, follow me" (Mt. 19:21).

This "come, follow me" is a central and culminating point of this whole episode. These words indicate that it is not possible to learn Christianity like a lesson composed of numerous different chapters, but that it must always be linked with a Person, a living Person: Jesus Christ. Jesus Christ is the guide: He is the model. We can imitate Him in different ways and to different extents. We can make Him, in different ways and to different extents, the "Rule" of our own lives.

Each of us is a kind of particular "material" from which—following Christ—we can draw this concrete, unique and absolutely individual form of life that can be called the Christian vocation. On this point, a great many things were said at the last Council as regards the vocation of the laity.

That does not change anything about the fact that this "follow me" of Christ's, in the precise case, is and remains the priestly vocation or the vocation to consecrated life according to the evangelical counsels. I say so because you asked the question (the 10th one) about my own priestly vocation. I will try to reply to you briefly, following the pattern of your question. So I will say first of all: I have been Pope for two years; I have been a bishop for over twenty years, and yet the most important thing for me still remains the fact of being a priest. The fact of being able to celebrate the Eucharist every day. Of being able to renew Christ's own sacrifice by giving back, in Him, all things to the Father: the world, humanity, and myself. The correct dimension of the Eucharist consists, in fact, in this. That is why I have always living in my memory this interior development as a result of which "I heard" Christ's call to the priesthood, this special "come and follow me."

Confiding this to you, I invite you to listen carefully, each one of you, to these evangelical words. It is in this way that your humanity will be formed completely, and that the Christian vocation of each of you will be defined. And perhaps you will also hear, in your turn, the call to the priesthood or to religious life. Until quite recently, France was rich in these vocations. She has given, among others, so many missionaries and so many missionary sisters to the Church! Certainly, Christ continues to speak on the banks of the Seine, and He always makes the same call. Listen attentively! It will always be necessary so that there may be in the Church those "chosen from among men," those whom Christ appoints, in a special way, on "behalf of men" (Heb. 5:1) and whom He sends to men.

You also asked the question about prayer (the 4th one). There are several definitions of prayer. But it is most often called a talk, a conversation, a colloquy with God. Conversing with someone, not only do we speak, but we also listen. Prayer, therefore, is also listening. It consists of listening to hear the interior voice of grace. Listening to hear the call. And then, as you ask me how the Pope prays, I answer you: like every Christian, he speaks and he listens. Sometimes, he prays without words, and then he listens all the more. The most important thing is precisely what he "hears." And he also tries to unite prayer with his obligations, his activities, his work, and to unite his work with prayer. In this way, day after day, he tries to carry out his "service," his "ministry," which comes to him from the will of Christ and from the living tradition of the Church.

You ask me, also, how I see this service now that I have already been, for two years, Peter's Successor (6th question). I see it above all as a maturation in the priesthood and as permanence in prayer, with Mary, the Mother of Christ, in the same way as the Apostles were assiduous in prayer, in the Upper Room in Jerusalem, when they received the Holy Spirit. In addition to that, you will find my answer to this question on the basis of the replies to the subsequent questions. And first and foremost, the one concerning the implementation of the Second Vatican Council (14th question). You ask if it is possible. And I reply to you: Not only is the implementation of the Council possible, but it is necessary. This answer is above all the answer of faith. It was the first answer I gave, on the day after my election, in the presence of the Cardinals gathered in the Sistine Chapel. It is the answer I gave myself and others, first as bishop and as Cardinal, and it is the answer I give continually. It is the main problem. I think that through the Council there were verified for the Church in our time the words of Christ in which He promised His Church the Spirit of truth, who will lead the minds and hearts of the Apostles and their successors, permitting them to remain in the truth and guide the Church in the truth, rereading "the signs of the times" in the light of this truth. That is precisely what the

Council did, in accordance with the needs of our time, of our age. I believe that, thanks to the Council, the Holy Spirit "is speaking" to the Church. I say that taking up again St. John's expression. Our duty is to understand firmly and honestly what "the Spirit says," and to carry it out, avoiding deviations from the road that the Council marked out from so many points of view.

The service of the bishop, and in particular that of the Pope, is bound up with a special responsibility as regards what the Spirit says: as regards the whole Faith of the Church and Christian morality. In fact, it is this Faith and this morality that they, the bishops with the Pope, must teach in the Church, watching by the light of tradition, always alive, over their conformity with the revealed Word of God. That is why they sometimes have to note also that certain opinions or certain publications show that they lack this conformity. They do not constitute an *authentic* doctrine of Christian faith and morality. I speak about this because you asked about it (5th question). If we had more time, a more developed exposition could be devoted to this problem—all the more so in that there is no lack of false information and erroneous explanations in this field, but today we must be content with these few words.

The work for the unity of Christians is, in my opinion, one of the greatest and finest tasks of the Church for our age.

You would like to know if I am expecting unity and how I view it. I will answer you the same thing as in connection with the implementation of the Council. There, too, I see a special call of the Holy Spirit. As regards its implementation, the different stages of this implementation, we find all the fundamental elements in the teaching of the Council. They must be put into practice, and their concrete applications must be sought; and above all it is necessary to pray always, with fervor, constancy and humility. The union of Christians cannot be realized otherwise than through deep maturation in the truth, and a constant conversion of hearts. We must do all that in accordance with our human capacities, taking up again all the "historical processes" that have lasted for centuries. But finally this union, for which we must spare no efforts or work, will be Christ's gift to His Church. Just as it is already one of His gifts that we have already entered upon the way to unity.

Continuing with the list of your questions, I reply to you: I have very often spoken of the duties of the Church in the field of justice and peace (15th question), thus continuing the activity of my great Predecessors John XXIII and Paul VI. Tomorrow in particular, I intend to speak at the headquarters of UNESCO, in Paris. I am referring to all that because you ask: what can we, the young, do for this cause? Can we do something to prevent a new war, a catastrophe that would be incomparable, more terrible than the preceding one? I think that, in the very formulation of your questions, you will find the awaited answer. Read these questions. Meditate on them. Make them a community program, a program of life. You young people have already the possibility of promoting peace and justice, where you are, in your world. That already comprises precise attitudes of kindness in judgment, truth about yourselves and others, their differences, and their important rights. In this way an atmosphere of brotherhood is prepared for the future when you will have greater responsibilities in society. If we wish to make a new and brotherly world, we must prepare new men.

And now the question on the Third World (the 8th one). It is a great question concerning history, culture and civilization. But it is above all a moral problem. You rightly ask what must be the relations between our country and the countries of the Third World: of Africa and Asia. There are, in fact, great obligations of a *moral nature* there. Our "western" world is at the same time "northern" (European or Atlantic). Its riches and its progress owe a great deal to the resources and men of these continents. In the new situation in which we find ourselves after the Council, it cannot seek there only sources of further riches and of its own progress. It must *consciously,* and by *organizing itself* to do so, serve their development. This is perhaps the most important problem as regards justice and peace in the world of today and tomorrow. The solution of this problem depends on the present generation, and it will depend on your generation and on those that will follow. Here, too, it is a question of continuing the witness borne to Christ and the Church by several previous generations of religious and lay missionaries.

The question: how to be a witness to Christ today? (18th one) This is the fundamental question, the continuation of the meditation we have placed at the center of our dialogue, the conversation with a young man. Christ says: "Follow me." This is what He said to Simon, the son of Jonas, to whom He gave the name of Peter; to his brother Andrew; to the sons of Zebedee; to Nathanael, He said, "follow me," repeating then, after the resurrection, "you shall be my witnesses" (Acts 1:8). To be a witness to Christ, to bear witness to Him, it is necessary, first, to follow Him. It is necessary to learn to know Him, to place oneself, so to speak, in His school, to penetrate all His mystery. It is a fundamental and central task. If we do not do so, if we are not ready to do so constantly and honestly, our witness runs the risk of becoming superficial and exterior. It runs the risk of no longer being witness. If, on the contrary, we remain attentive to that, Christ Himself will teach us, through His Spirit, what we have to do, how to behave, in what and how to commit ourselves, how to carry on the dialogue with the modern world; this dialogue that Paul VI called the dialogue of salvation.

If you ask me consequently: "What must we do in the Church, we above all, the young?" I will reply: learn to know Christ. Constantly. To learn Christ. The unfathomable treasures of wisdom and science are really found in Him. In Him, man, on whom there weigh his limits, his vices, his weakness and his sin, really becomes "the new man": he becomes the man "for others," he also becomes the glory of God, because the glory of God, as St. Irenaeus of Lyons, bishop and martyr, said in the second century, is "living man." The experience of two millennia teaches us that in this fundamental work, the mission of the whole People of God, there is no essential difference between man and woman. Each in his way, according to the specific characteristics of femininity and masculinity, becomes this "new man," that is, this man "for others," and as a living man he becomes the glory of God. If that is true, just as it is true that the Church, in the hierarchical sense, is directed by the successors of the Apostles and therefore by men, it is certainly all the more true that, in the charismatic sense, women "lead" her as much, and perhaps even more: I invite you to think often of Mary, the Mother of Christ.

Before concluding this testimony based on your questions, I would like to thank again very specially the many representatives of French youth who, before my arrival in Paris, sent me thousands of letters. I thank you for having manifested this bond, this communion, this co-responsibility. I hope that this bond, this communion and this co-responsibility will be continued, and will deepen and develop after our meeting this evening.

I ask you also to strengthen your union with the young people of the whole Church·and of the world, in the spirit of this certainty that Christ is our Way, the Truth and the Life (cf. Jn. 14:6).

Let us now unite in this prayer which He Himself taught us, singing "Our Father," and receive, all of you, for yourselves, for boys and girls of your age, for your families and for those who are suffering most, the blessing of the Bishop of Rome, the Successor of St. Peter.

Our Father who art in heaven, hallowed be thy name. Thy kingdom come, thy will be done, on earth as it is in heaven. Give us this day our daily bread, and forgive us our trespasses, as we forgive those who trespass against us; and lead us not into temptation, but deliver us from evil. Amen.

"Ah, If You Could Realize the Hope That Is in You"

On June 1, 1980, after his address to the French bishops, the Holy Father went to the auditorium of the Seminary at Issy les Moulineaux where he met the 220 seminarians and numerous members of the priests' councils of the Paris region. He spoke to them as follows.

Dear seminarian friends,

I could not conclude this afternoon without spending a moment with you, getting to know your faces, and exhorting you in the name of the Lord. What joy to meet you, you young students in formation in the Paris region! I have been told that there are gathered here the students of the St. Sulpice Seminary, those of the University Seminary of the Carmelites and members of different preparatory groups. Fine. I am happy that it is possible to count on your availability to serve, on your generosity. Addressing these few words to you, you will allow me to address at the same time all your French confreres who, elsewhere in this country, but also in my diocese of Rome, are following the same way.

As you know, I have just had a long working-session with your bishops. It was a particularly important conversation, in the course of which we were able, we who are jointly in charge of all the churches, to face up to our responsibilities in order to assume them according to what pleases God. And now, it seems quite natural to continue this conversation, in a way, with those who are preparing to become collaborators of the episcopal order, and to be associated in this way, in the person of Christ, with the preaching of the Gospel and the guidance of the People of God. You are still young, certainly, but already you divine a great many things. You understand that your gift must be complete and that, the further you go, the more you will discover the necessity of making it—if I may venture to say so—even more complete. It is at this level, therefore, that I will take up my position with you, taking into account, of course, the fact that a way such as yours takes time, and a long spiritual, intellectual and pastoral maturation, and that the mere desire to become a priest is not enough in itself to meet the requirements of the priesthood.

Discover the Sense of Self-Sacrifice

One of these requirements, the most fundamental one, is that you should be deeply rooted in Jesus Christ. I invite you to this with all my heart. If you could learn, through prayer and contemplation, to live, preach, love and suffer like Christ, it seems that the main lines of your mission would gradually take shape clearly, and that you would also feel a vital need to join men and bring them what they really need. In such a proceeding there is already the soul of the apostolate, so that "action" is indissolubly linked with "being," and vice-versa. Here it is not useful to pursue vain discussions, nor is it good to prefer one to the detriment of the other. The Church intends to form you in complete interior unity, in which the mission requires intimacy with God, and in which the latter calls for the former.

Do you not want to be, yourselves, "good shepherds"? The good shepherd gives his life, and he gives his life for his sheep. Very well, then! It is necessary to discover the sense of self-sacrifice, linked with the sacrifice of Christ, and offer yourselves for others, who expect this witness from you. That can be said of all the faithful, but with all the more reason and in a very special way of priests and future priests. May your daily participation in the Eucharist and the efforts you make to increase Eucharistic devotion within you, help you along this way!

Pastoral Wisdom

I was speaking to you a moment ago of unity among yourselves. In my opinion, it makes it possible to acquire what could be called pastoral wisdom. One of the fruits of the conciliar decree of Vatican II on the formation of priests was certainly to create the conditions for better pastoral preparation of candidates. Thanks to the inner balance you achieve, you must be able to improve your judgment of men, things and situations, and view them in the light of God and not with the eyes of the world. That will lead you to a deep perception of the problems, and of the multiple urgent needs of the mission, and at the same time that will urge you on towards the right goal. In this way you will be less exposed to the temptation of "extolling" only what our contemporaries are living, or on the contrary of experimenting on them, pastoral ideas that are perhaps generous, but personal and without the guarantee of the Church: there must be no experimenting on men. You will take to heart, for this very reason, your intellectual work, indispensable today as it is after ordination, in order to transmit to others the whole content of faith in an exact, harmonious synthesis, easy to assimilate.

Is it necessary, besides, to point out that the priest is one among others? By himself, he cannot be everything to everyone. His ministry is exercised within a presbyterium, around a bishop. Such already in a small way is your own case, to the extent that your bonds with your diocese where you are integrated in the pastoral teams to develop in you the capacity of working as a Church, are gradually strengthened. And if your personal path—or the stress sometimes laid on such and such an aspect of your preparation—make you more suitable for a given type of ministry, among a more particular category of the population, nevertheless you will be sent basically to everyone, with pastoral concern for everyone and the determination to collaborate with everyone, excluding no trend or environment. You must be capable also of accepting any ministry that is entrusted to you, without subordinating your acceptance to conformity with expediency or personal projects. In this matter, it is the needs of the Church that have priority, and it is necessary to adapt oneself to them. This seems absolutely essential to your bishops and myself, in consideration of the office with which Providence has invested us and with which you will be associated one day.

With Faith and Joy

My dear sons, you see the vastness of the task, the vastness of the needs. You are not very numerous, and yet the efforts undertaken for several years are beginning to yield visible results. I shall not tell you that the generosity of the laity will make it possible to mitigate the lack of priests. It is completely of another order. In the laity you will always have to develop the sense of responsibility and to educate them to take their full place in the community. But what God has put in your hearts through His call corresponds to a specific vocation. Try to bear witness better to your faith and your joy. You are the witnesses of priestly vocations among adolescents and young people of your age. Ah! If you could realize the hope that is in you, and show that the mission cannot wait, in France and even more in other less privileged countries! I encourage you with all my strength to be the first apostles of vocations.

Priests of Quality

I also wish to encourage and thank your teachers and educators at all levels: rectors of seminaries, diocesan delegates, parish priests, chaplaincies and movements which contribute to your formation, and those who enabled you to discern the Lord's call. You owe them a great deal. The Church owes them a great deal. In this place, I would like to pay tribute especially to priests of the Society of St. Sulpice, who have won the esteem of everyone in their service of the priesthood.

Your educators have a difficult task. It must be known, in France, that I put my trust in them and give them my brotherly support. They wish to form priests of quality. May they continue their efforts and develop them further, with the help of the texts of the Council, the excellent *Rationes* which have been prepared at the request of the Holy See, and the recent documents published by the Congregation for Catholic Education, which they have, I do not doubt, distributed widely among you and commented upon.

My hearty thanks to you all, dear confreres and dear sons. I shall see you later, at the Parc des Princes, with the young people of the Paris region, and I bless you with my deep affection.

In the Name of the Love I Bear You!

The address prepared by the Holy Father for the meeting with young Parisians at Parc des Princes, on June 1, 1980, which was replaced by the one that the Pope actually delivered in reply to the questions submitted to him, was left to the young in the form of a message. The text is as follows:

Thank you, thank you, dear young people of France, for having come this evening for this vigil with the Pope! Thank you for your trust! I thank, too, all those who have written to me! The meeting with the young is always a very special moment of my pastoral visits. Thank you for what you have prepared this evening for the eyes and for the heart! You now give me your testimony, you profess your faith. And I will then speak of your lives as young people, bearing in mind your questions, and with you I will profess the whole faith of the Church.

Dear young people of France,

My hearty thanks for having come in such large numbers, so joyful, so confident, so united with one another! My thanks to the young people of Paris and of the Paris region! My thanks to the young people who have come enthusiastically from all over France! I would have liked so much to shake hands with each of you, look into your eyes, and say a personal and friendly word. This practical impossibility is not an obstacle to the deep communion of spirits and hearts. Your exchanges of testimonies are the proof.

Your assembly is a delight to my eyes and overwhelms my heart. Your assembly of young people has wished to be worthy of the crowds of young people I have already met in the course of my apostolic journeys, in Mexico first of all, then in Poland, in Ireland, in the United States, and recently in Africa. I can confide to you: God has bestowed on me—as on so many bishops and priests—the grace of loving the young passionately. Though they are certainly different from one country to another, they are so similar in their enthusiasms and their disappointments, their aspirations and their generosity!

Those of you who have had the possibility of establishing contacts and making friends with young people of another province, another country, another continent than their own, will understand better, perhaps, and certainly share my faith in youth, because it is everywhere, today as yesterday, the bearer of great hopes for the world and for the Church. Young people of France, convinced Christians or sympathizers with Christianity, I would like us, on this unforgettable evening, to make a climb, all roped together, in the direction of the difficult, and at the same time bracing, peaks of the vocation of man, of Christian man. I wish, in fact, to share with you, as a friend with his friends, my own convictions as a man and as a servant of the faith and unity of the People of God.

An Existence Really Human

Your problems and your sufferings as young people are known to me, at least in general: a certain instability inherent in your age and increased by the acceleration of the changes of history, a certain mistrust with regard to certainties, aggravated by the knowledge learned at school and the frequent atmosphere of systematic criticism, concern about the future and the difficulties of professional integration, the stimulation and superabundance of desires in a society which makes pleasure the purpose of life, the painful feeling of powerlessness to master the ambiguous or fatal consequences of progress, the temptations of revolt, escape or resignation. You know all that, to the extent of being saturated with it. I prefer, with you, to reach the heights. I am convinced that you want to get out of this debilitating atmosphere and deepen or rediscover the meaning of an existence that is really human because it is open to God, in a word, your vocation as a man in Christ.

The human being is a corporeal being. This very simple statement is pregnant with consequences. However material it may be, the body is not an object among other objects. It is in the first place some one, in the sense that it is a manifestation of the person, a way of being present to others, of communication, of extremely varied expression. The body is a word, a language. What a marvel, and what a risk at the same time! Young men and women, have very great respect for your body and for the bodies of others! Let your body be in the service of your inner self! Let your gestures, your looks, always be the reflection of your soul! Worship of the body? No, never! Contempt for the body? Again no! Control of the body? Yes! Transfiguration of the body! Even more! It often happens to you to admire the marvelous transparency of the soul in many men and women in the daily accomplishment of their human tasks. Think of the student or sportsman who put all their physical energies in the service of their respective ideal. Think of the father and the mother whose faces, bending over their child, reveal so deeply the joys of fatherhood and mother- hood. Think of the musician or the actor identified with the authors whom they bring to life again. See the Trappist or the Carthusian, the Carmelite or the Poor Clare, radically abandoned to contemplation and letting God shine through them.

Mastery of Self

I really hope that you will take up the challenge of this time and be, one and all, champions of Christian mastery of the body. Sport rightly understood, which is springing up again today beyond the circle of professionals, is a very great help. This mastery is decisive for the integration of sexuality in your lives as young people and adults. It is difficult to speak of sexuality at the present time, marked by a lack of inhibitions which is not without an explanation but which is, alas, stimulated by a real exploitation of the sexual instinct. Young people of France, the union of bodies has always been the most forceful language in which two beings can communicate with each other. That is why this language, which touches the sacred mystery of man and woman, demands that the gestures of love should never be performed without the conditions of a complete and definitive assumption of responsibility for the partner, and that the commitment should be undertaken publicly in marriage. Young people of France, preserve or find again a healthy view of corporal values! Contemplate more Christ the Redeemer of man! He is the Word made flesh whom so many artists have painted with realism in order to signify to us clearly that He assumed everything of human nature, including sexuality, sublimating it in chastity.

A Mind To Think

The mind is the original element that fundamentally distinguishes man from the animal world and that gives him the power to master the universe. I cannot resist quoting to you your incomparable French writer, Pascal: "Man is only a reed, the weakest one in nature; but he is a thinking reed. It is not necessary for the whole universe to take up arms to crush him...; but even if the universe were to crush him, man would still be nobler than what kills him, because he knows that he is dying; and the universe knows nothing of the advantage it has over him. Our whole dignity, therefore, consists in thought...; so let us work at thinking well" (*Pensées,* no. 347).

Speaking of the mind in this way, I mean the mind capable of understanding, willing, loving. It is precisely through these that man is a man. Safeguard the sacred sphere of the mind at all costs in you and around you! You know that in the modern world there still exist, alas, totalitarian systems which paralyze the mind, and seriously impair the integrity, the identity of man, by reducing him to the state of an object, a machine, by depriving him of his interior resilience, of his impulses of freedom and love. You know also that there are economic systems which, while priding themselves on their formidable industrial expansion, accentuate, at the same time, the degradation, the decomposition of man. Even the mass media, which should contribute to the complete development of men and to their mutual enrichment in growing brotherhood, are sometimes guilty of hammering at the intelligence and the imagination and even bewitching them, in a way that is harmful to the health of the mind, of judgment and of the heart, and distorts man's capacity of discerning what is healthy from what is unhealthy.

Yes, what is the use of social and political reforms, even very generous ones, if the mind, which is also conscience, loses its lucidity and its vigor? In practice, in the world such as it is and which you must not flee, learn more and more to reflect, to think! The studies that you are carrying out must be a very special moment of apprenticeship to the life of the mind. Unmask slogans, false values, mirages, dead ends! I wish you the spirit of meditation, of interiority. Each one of you, at his or her level, must promote the primacy of the spirit and even contribute to bringing back into honor what has value for eternity even more than for the future. Living in this way, believers or non-believers, you are all close to God. God is Spirit!

A Heart To Love

You are also worth what your heart is worth. The whole history of mankind is the history of the need of loving and being loved. This end of the century—especially in regions of accelerated social change—makes the development of healthy emotions more difficult. That is probably why many young and not so young people seek the atmosphere of little groups, in order to escape from anonymity and sometimes from distress, in order to find again their deep vocation for interpersonal relations. If we are to believe a certain type of advertising, our age is even enamored of what could be called a doping of the heart.

It is important in this sphere, as in the preceding ones, to see things clearly. Whatever use humans make of it, the heart—the symbol of friendship and love—has also its norms, its ethics. To make room for the heart in the harmonious construction of your personality has nothing to do with mawkishness or even sentimentality. The heart is the opening of the whole being to the existence of others, the capacity of divining them, of understanding them. Such a sensitiveness, true and deep, makes one vulnerable. That is why some people are tempted to get rid of it by hardening their heart.

To love is, therefore, essentially to give oneself to others. Far from being an instinctive inclination, love is a conscious decision of the will to go towards others. To be able to love truly, it is necessary to detach oneself from many things and above all from oneself, to give gratuitously, to love to the end. This dispossession of oneself—a long and demanding task—is exhausting and exalting. It is the source of balance. It is the secret of happiness.

Young people of France, raise your eyes more often towards Jesus Christ! He is the Man who loved most, and most consciously, most voluntarily and most gratuitously! Meditate on Christ's testament: "There is no greater proof of love than to give one's life for those one loves." Contemplate the Man-God, the man with the pierced heart! Do not be afraid! Jesus did not come to condemn love but to free love from its ambiguities and its counterfeits. It was He who changed the heart of Zacchaeus, of the Samaritan woman, and who still operates similar conversions today, all over the world. It seems to me that tonight, Christ is whispering to each one of you: "Give me your heart!... I will purify it, I will strengthen it, I will turn it towards all those who need it: towards your own family, your school or university community, your social environment, towards the unloved, towards foreigners living on the soil of France, towards the inhabitants of the Third World who do not have enough to live on and to develop, towards the most humble of men. Love demands sharing!"

Young people of France, it is more than ever the time to work hand-in-hand at the civilization of love, according to the expression dear to my great Predecessor, Paul VI. What a gigantic workyard! What a stirring task!

On the plane of the heart of love, I have something else to confide to you. I believe with my whole strength that many of you are capable of risking the complete gift, to

Christ and to their brothers, of all their powers of loving. You understand perfectly that I mean the vocation to the priesthood and to religious life. Your towns and villages in France are waiting for ministers with hearts burning to proclaim the Gospel, celebrate the Eucharist, reconcile sinners with God and with their brothers. They are also waiting for women radically consecrated to the service of Christian communities and their human and spiritual needs. Your answer to this call lies along the direct line of Christ's last question to Peter: "Do you love me?"

The Mystery of Christ's Love for Us

I have spoken of the values of the heart, the mind and the heart. But at the same time I have given glimpses of an essential dimension without which man becomes again a prisoner of himself or of others: it is openness to God. Yes, without God, man loses the key to himself, he loses the key to his history. For, since creation, he has borne within him the likeness of God. This remains in him in the state of an implicit wish and unconscious need, in spite of sin. And man is destined to live with God. There, too, Christ will reveal Himself as our way. But this mystery requires, perhaps, greater attention.

Jesus Christ, the Son of God made man, lived everything that constitutes the value of our human nature, body, mind and heart, in a fully free relationship with others, marked by the seal of truth and filled with love. His whole life, as much as His words, manifested this freedom, this truth, this love, and especially the voluntary gift of His life for men. In this way He was able to proclaim the charter of a blessed world, yes blessed, on the way of poverty, sweetness, justice, hope, mercy, purity, peace, faithfulness, even in persecution, and two thousand years afterwards, this charter is inscribed in the heart of our gathering. But Christ did not only give an example and teach. He actually freed men and women from what held their bodies, their minds and their hearts captive. And since His death and resurrection for us, He continues to do so, for men and women from all walks of life and from all countries, from the moment when they give Him their faith. He is the Savior of man. He is the Redeemer of man. *"Ecce homo,"* Pilate said, without being clearly conscious of the significance of his words: "there is the man."

How do we dare to say that, dear friends? Christ's earthly life was a short one, His public life even shorter. But His life is unique, His personality is unique in the world. He is not only a Brother for us, a Friend, a Man of God. We recognize in Him the only Son of God, who is one with God the Father and whom the Father gave to the world. With the apostle Peter, whose humble Successor I am, I profess: "You are the Christ, the Son of the living God." It is precisely because Christ shares at once the divine nature and our human nature that the offering of His life, in His death and His resurrection, reaches us, the men of today, saves us, purifies us, frees us, elevates us: "The Son of God in a certain way united Himself with each man." And I like to repeat here the wish of my first encyclical: "That each person may be able to find Christ, in order that Christ may walk with each person the path of life, with the power of the truth about man and the world that is contained in the mystery of the Incarnation and the redemption and with the power of the love that is radiated by that truth" (*Redemptor hominis*, no. 13).

If Christ liberates and raises our humanity, it is because He introduces it into the covenant with God, with the Father, with the Son, and with the Holy Spirit. This morning we celebrated the feast of the Holy Trinity. That is the real opening to God to which every human heart aspires even without knowing it and which Christ offers the believer. It is a question of a personal God and not just the God of philosophers and scholars; it is the God revealed in the Bible, the God of Abraham, the God of Jesus Christ, He who is at the heart of our history. He is the God who can seize all the resources of your body, your mind and your heart, to make them bear fruit, in a word, who can seize your whole being to renew it in Christ, now and beyond death.

That is my faith, that has been the faith of the Church since its origin, the only one that is founded on the witness of the Apostles, the only one that resists fluctuations, the only one that saves man. I am sure that many of you have already experienced it. May they find in my coming an encouragement to deepen it by all the means that the Church puts at their disposal.

Others are undoubtedly more hesitant to adhere fully to this faith. Some consider themselves to be unbelievers and perhaps incapable of believing, or indifferent to faith. Others still reject a God whose face has been badly presented to them. Others, finally, shaken by the fall-out of philosophies of suspicion which present religion as an illusion or alienation, are perhaps tempted to construct a humanism without God. I hope, however, that all those will at least, out of honesty, leave their window open to God. Otherwise they run the risk of missing the way to man which Christ is, of shutting themselves up in attitudes of revolt and violence, of contenting themselves with sighs of helplessness or resignation. A world without God is constructed, sooner or later, against man. Certainly, many social or cultural influences, many personal events, may have obstructed your way to faith, or turned you away from it. But actually, if you wish, in the midst of these difficulties which I understand, you have still, finally, a good chance, in your country of religious freedom, to clear this way and have access, with the grace of God, to faith! You have the means to do so! Are you really taking them? In the name of all the love that I bear you, I do not hesitate to call upon you: "Throw open your doors to Christ!" What do you fear? Trust Him. Take the risk of following Him. That requires, of course, that you should come out of yourselves, your reasonings, your "wisdom," your indifference, your self-complacency, the non-Christian habits that you may have acquired. Yes, that calls for sacrifice, a conversion, which you must first dare to desire, ask in prayer and begin to practice. Let Christ be for you the Way, the Truth, and the Life. Let Him be your salvation and your happiness. Let Him seize your whole life in order that it may reach all its dimensions with Him, that all your relationships, activities, feelings and thoughts may be integrated in Him, one could say "Christified." I hope that with Christ you will recognize God as the source and end of your existence.

These are the men and women that the world needs, that France needs. You will personally have the happiness promised in the beatitudes and you will be, in all humility and respect for others, and in their midst, the leaven of which the Gospel speaks. You will build a new world; you will prepare a Christian future. It is a way of the cross, yes, it is also a way of joy, for it is a way of hope.

With all my trust and all my affection I call upon the young people of France to raise their heads and walk together along this way, their hands in the Lord's hand. "Arise, young woman! Arise, young man!"

"Interior Certainty"

During the general audience of June 4, 1980, Pope John Paul II urged the young people to be joyful and strong in their faith in Jesus Christ.

Beloved young people, to you I address the biblical invitation of the book of Ecclesiastes: "Rejoice, O young man, in your youth, and let your heart cheer you in the days of your youth.... Remove vexation from your mind" (Eccl. 11:9-10). Be joyful in the Lord Jesus, because He has conquered the world and what is of the world: "the lust of the flesh and the lust of the eyes and the pride of life" (1 Jn. 2:16), and He continually communicates His victory to you by means of faith in His word, and makes you strong (cf. 1 Jn. 2:14). May this interior certainty nourish your serenity, give a foundation to your joy, and offer support to your confidence in the future. With my blessing.

Open to Grace!

Pope John Paul II addressed an affectionate greeting to the young present at the general audience of June 11, 1980. His Holiness pleaded with them to heed the call to the priestly or religious vocation.

Your presence, dear young people, brings back to my mind the episode of that young man of the Gospel (cf. Mt. 19:16ff.) who presented himself to Jesus, asking Him what he should do to have eternal life.

—Observe the commandments!

—I have observed them from my childhood. What else must I do?

And Jesus, looking at him lovingly, as I am now looking at you, replied:

—If you would be perfect, go, sell what you possess and give it to the poor. Then come and follow me.

Dear young people, there are two steps that the Church has always proposed to the most generous hearts: observance of the commandments; and, for the strongest, voluntary renunciation of even the most legitimate goods and affections to serve Him with unlimited freedom of heart. Do not close your ears to these promptings of grace!

Always and Everywhere a Christian

At the general audience of June 18, 1980, Pope John Paul exhorted the young to be faithful Christians during vacation time and always.

I now address a very cordial greeting to all the young, to the boys and girls taking part in this audience. Beloved in Christ, your schoolwork is ended or about to end, and the holidays are awaiting you. It is right that you should rest and enjoy yourselves; but the Pope urges you also never to forget your religious commitments. The Christian is always and everywhere a Christian: at home, at school, at work, at rest, in enjoyment. May St. Aloysius Gonzaga, whose feast-day we will celebrate in a few days, help you to be faithful to the Christian vocation. With this wish I willingly bless you.

Christ, the Light of Your Souls

On June 21, 1980, thousands of young people of Catholic Action carried out a torchlight procession in St. Peter's Square on the occasion of the fifteenth anniversary of the closing of the Second Vatican Council. The Holy Father delivered the following address from the window of his private study.

Dear young people! Girls and boys!

You have come to St. Peter's Square carrying these burning torches to manifest the fundamental truth about yourselves.

These torches speak of your hearts.

These torches speak of your lives.

They say that you cannot and will not walk in the darkness, that you need light. In fact, that you wish to carry light to illuminate the ways of your lives and the lives of others.

You profess that this light is Christ; that He is the Light of human souls. He is the Light of your young souls. He shows God to man: He who sees Christ, sees the Father at the same time (cf. Jn. 14:9). And He shows man to man. The mystery of man—sometimes so obscure and misty—is illuminated in Him. Christ proclaims the Good News. He proclaims it in Himself, in His own life, by the cross and resurrection. He teaches how great is man's dignity, how great is his calling.

You who have discovered this truth must take it in your hands like a lamp that is lit. And you must keep watch!

First of all you must keep watch so that this light will not be extinguished in you. That it will not be smothered or even driven away, either by any breath of contrary wind coming from outside, or by the lack of fuel in yourselves, in your hearts.

At the same time you must keep watch in the place of others and for others. For so many generations, for so many centuries, Christ has been passing along the streets of this earth, of Italy—and of this city, Rome....

And He always comes as the Bridegroom, as the One who loved man to the point of the complete offering of Himself.

May He not pass in vain!

May more and more men meet Him!

May those of your own age meet Him, in ever larger numbers!

May you yourselves be able to show them the way that leads to Christ!

For this I pray today together with you. And from the heart of this prayer I bestow on you my blessing in the name of the Blessed Trinity.

May your hearts be open!

May the lamps in your hands be lit!

Keep watch!

Innocence and Friendship with Jesus

On June 25, 1980, the Holy Father addressed a special word to the first communicants and other young people who had gone to the general audience.

I now address a special greeting to you, children, boys and girls and young people, who, with such enthusiasm and exuberance, have wished to come to this audience to see the Pope and thus manifest your faith in Jesus Christ, represented here by His Vicar. I greet particularly those boys and girls among you who have just approached the Sacrament of the Eucharist, in First Communion, and still bear with them the perfume of the eucharistic bread and the fragrance of Jesus' love for us. I wish you all to be able to preserve always the grace, the light and the smile derived from innocence and from friendship with Jesus.

Build Your Future on the Foundation of Christ!

About 11:30 a.m., on July 1, 1980, John Paul II arrived at Belo Horizonte, Brazil. He drove in an open car across the city and was given a rapturous welcome by the population. On arrival at the Praca Israel Pinheiro on the outskirts of the city, he celebrated Mass there for youth and for students. The following is the text of his homily.

Dear young people and my friends,

Do not be surprised if the Pope begins this homily with a confession. I had read many times that half of the population of your country is under twenty-five years of age. Contemplating from my arrival at Brasilia, wherever I went, an infinity of young faces; passing amid multitudes of young people, on reaching this city; seeing you young people in such large numbers round this altar, I confess that I have understood better, from this concrete sight, what I had learned in an abstract way. I think that I have also understood better why the bishops of Puebla speak of a preferential option—not an exclusive one, certainly, but a priority one—for the young.

This option means that the Church assumes the commitment of continually proclaiming a message of full liberation to the young.

It is the message of salvation that she hears from the mouth of the Savior Himself and that she must transmit with absolute faithfulness.

You Must Bear Witness

At this Mass that I have the joy of celebrating in your midst and for your intentions, this message appears in its essential content from the readings we have just heard.

"Keep justice and do righteousness," the Prophet Isaiah exhorts us with a forcefulness that is not exhausted 2,500 years afterwards (Is. 56:1). And he adds: it is important above all to "hold fast my covenant," the covenant that God sealed with man. It is an invitation to consistency and faithfulness, an invitation that concerns the young very closely.

In Paul's letter to the Christians of Corinth, we heard strong and convincing words as those of the great Apostle usually are: whoever wishes to construct his life must not lay a foundation other than that which has already been laid: Christ Jesus (cf. 1 Cor. 3:10). Paul knew very well what he was saying. As an adolescent, he had persecuted the Church. But one fine day on the way to Damascus there was that unexpected meeting with Jesus in person. And it is the testimony of his own life that makes him say: there is no other foundation possible. It is urgent to place Jesus as the foundation of existence.

In the Gospel of St. Matthew, there is that page that no one can reread without emotion. Jesus asks the Apostles: "Who do men say that the Son of man is?" After they have reported a series of opinions, the fundamental question comes: "But who do you say that I am?" We all know this moment, in which it is no longer sufficient to speak about Jesus repeating what others have said. You must say what you think, and not quote an opinion. You must bear witness, feel committed by the witness you have borne and carry this commitment to its extreme consequences. The best friends, followers and apostles of Christ have always been those who heard within them one day the definitive, unescapable question, before which all others become secondary and derivative: "For you, who am I?" The life, the destiny, the present and future history of a young person depends on the clear and sincere answer, without rhetoric or subterfuges, that he gives to this question. It has already changed the lives of many young people.

The Church Looks to You

It is from these messages offered by the Word of God that I would like to draw a simple and straightforward message to leave with you at this meeting, which enables me to feel the seriousness with which you are facing up to your lives.

The greatest wealth of this country, which is immensely rich, is you. The real future of this "Country of the future" is enclosed in the presence of you young people. Therefore, this country, and with it the Church, looks to you with expectation and hope.

Open to the social dimensions of man, you do not conceal your determination to change radically the social structures that you consider unjust. You say, rightly, that it is impossible to be happy when you see a multitude of brothers who lack the minimum required for a life worthy of man. You also say that it is not right that some people should waste what is lacking on the table of others. You are resolved to construct a just, free and prosperous society, in which one and all will be able to enjoy the benefits of progress.

Tremendous Experience

In my youth I lived these same convictions. As a young student, I proclaimed them with the voice of literature and art.

God willed that they should be tempered in the fire of a war whose atrocity did not spare my family. I saw these convictions trampled upon in many ways. I feared for them, seeing them exposed to the tempest. One day I decided to confront them with Jesus Christ: I realized that He was the only one who revealed to me their real content and value and that in this way I could protect them against the inevitable wear and tear of time, in its mysterious workings.

All this, this tremendous and precious experience, taught me that social justice is true only if it is based on the rights of the individual. And that these rights will be really recognized only if we recognize the transcendent dimension of man, created in the image and likeness of God, called to be His son and the brother of other men, and destined to eternal life. To deny this transcendency is to reduce man to an instrument of domination, whose fate is subject to the selfishness and ambition of other men, or to the omnipotence of the totalitarian state erected as the supreme value.

In the same interior movement that led me to the discovery of Jesus Christ and drew me irresistibly to Him, I perceived something that the Second Vatican Council expressed clearly much later. I realized that "the Gospel (of Christ) announces and proclaims the freedom of the sons of God, it rejects all bondage resulting from sin, it scrupulously respects the dignity of conscience and its freedom of choice, it never ceases to encourage the employment of human talents in the service of God and man, and finally, it commends everyone to the charity of all. This is nothing other than the basic law of the Christian scheme of things" (Const. *Gaudium et spes*, no. 41).

Holding to Convictions

I learned that a young Christian ceases to be young, and has no longer been a Christian for a long time, when he lets himself be won over by doctrines or ideologies that preach hatred and violence. For a just society cannot be constructed on injustice. It is not possible to construct a society that deserves to be called human without respecting and, worse still, by destroying, human freedom, denying individuals the most fundamental freedoms.

Sharing as priest, bishop and Cardinal the lives of innumerable young people at the University, in youth groups, in excursions in the mountains, in clubs for reflection and prayer, I learned that a youth begins to grow old in a dangerous way, when he lets himself be deceived by the facile and convenient principle that "the end justifies the means"; when he adopts the belief that the only hope of improving society is to promote struggle and hatred between social groups, that it is to be found in the Utopia of a classless society, which very soon reveals itself as the creator of new classes. I became convinced that only love draws closer things that are different, and brings about union in diversity. Christ's words: "A new commandment I give to you, that you love one another; even as I have loved you" (Jn. 13:34), then appeared to me, in addition to their incomparable theological depth, as the seed and principle of the one transformation radical enough to be appreciated by the young. The seed and principle of the one revolution that does not betray man. Only true love constructs.

Know What You Want

If a young man such as I was, called to live his youth at a crucial moment of history, can say something to young people like you, I think he would say to them: Do not let yourselves be used!

Try to be clearly aware of what you want and what you do. But I see that this is just what the bishops of Latin America said to you, when they were gathered in Puebla last year: "There will be formed in the young a critical sense before...the cultural countervalues that the various ideologies try to transmit to them" (Puebla Document, no. 1197), particularly ideologies of a materialistic character, so that they will not be manipulated by them. And the Second Vatican Council: "The social order requires constant improvement: it must be founded in truth, built on justice and enlivened by love: it should grow in freedom towards a more humane equilibrium" (Const. *Gaudium et spes,* no. 26).

A great Predecessor of mine, Pope Pius XII, took as his motto: "To construct peace in justice." I think it is a motto and above all a commitment worthy of you, young Brazilians!

Overcome Temptations

I am afraid that many good desires to construct a just society flounder on the lack of authenticity and burst like a bubble when they are not sustained by a serious commitment of austerity and frugality. In other words, it is necessary to overcome the temptation of the so-called "consumer society," the temptation of the ambition to *have* more and more, instead of trying to *be* more and more; the ambition to have more and more, while others have less and less. In this connection, I think that the beatitude of the poor in spirit should take on concrete meaning and power in your lives: in the rich young man, so that he will understand that the superfluous things he has are nearly always what others lack, and that he may not go away sorrowfully (cf. Mt. 19:22) if he hears in the depths of his conscience a call of the Lord to fuller detachment; in the young man who is living the hard experience of uncertainty of the future, who may even suffer the pangs of hunger, so that, seeking to improve, as is right, the living standards of his family and of himself, he may be attracted by human dignity, not by ambition, greed, and the fascination of the superfluous.

My friends, you are also responsible for the preservation of the real values that have always done honor to the Brazilian people. Do not let yourselves be swept away by the provocation of sex, which compromises the authenticity of human love and leads to the disintegration of the family. "Do you not know that you are God's temple and that God's Spirit dwells in you?" St. Paul wrote in the text we have heard read to us.

Let girls try to find true *feminism*, the real fulfillment of woman as a human person, as an integral part of the family and as a member of society, in conscious participation, according to her characteristics.

Build on Jesus Christ

In conclusion, I take up again the key words we have gathered from the readings of this Mass: Do what you should do and practice righteousness; do not build on any foundation other than Jesus Christ; have an answer to give the Lord when He asks: "For you, who am I?"

This is the sincere and trustful message of a friend. My desire would be to shake hands with each of you and speak to each one.

In any case, I say to one and all: young people of Belo Horizonte and of the whole of Brazil, the Pope loves you!

The Pope will never forget you! The Pope takes away from here a great yearning for you!

Receive, dear friends, the apostolic blessing that I shall give you at the end of this Mass, as a sign of my friendship, of my confidence in you, and in all the young people of this country.

Before going on to the eucharistic liturgy properly speaking, just one more word: Only love builds, only love brings close, only love unites men in their diversity.

Recently I was in France, and there the young people I met asked me spontaneously to bring you some messages of friendship, which I was very happy to do. May this gesture of the outstretched hand serve as a symbol and stimulus to construct human, Christian and ecclesial brotherhood more and more in the world.

"Where are you going?" With you I ask this question; with you, dear young people, I am about to offer also all that is noble in your hearts, all the beautiful experience we are living here together, for the success of the Eucharistic Congress of Fortaleza, to which I am going as a pilgrim, together with the Church in Brazil.

"Where are you going?" Amen.

Listening to the Lord, the Great Friend

On July 5, 1980, the Pope met over ten thousand priests and "voca-cionados," that is, all those who feel "called" to the priesthood or religious life, most of whom came from the State of Rio Grande do Sul, Brazil, but many also from the State of Santa Catarina, as well as from Uruguay, Paraguay, Argentina, and Chile. The Holy Father delivered the following address.

Beloved sons,

You will certainly not be surprised if I confide to you that this meeting was one of those most anticipated by me among the many that Providence grants me in this great nation. It is a joy to be able to meet you young people, ready to follow Jesus Christ, who calls for a complete gift of oneself in witness to love for Him and service for brothers; with you priests and religious who are responsible for the formation of those preparing for the priesthood, religious life, or a direct commitment in apostolic activity. On you there depends to a great extent the future of the Church in Brazil.

"Grace to you and peace from God the Father and the Lord Jesus Christ" (2 Thes. 1:2). Many thanks for the cordiality and enthusiasm of your welcome, which I greatly appreciate. It is another expression of the traditional Brazilian hospitality that I have experienced in these days.

At every moment of this pastoral pilgrimage of mine through your land, with my heart turned to Fortaleza and in harmony with the People of God in Brazil, I ask myself: "Where are you going?" The mouth speaks from the abundance of the heart. In all the stages of my pilgrimage to the National Eucharistic Congress, the question was, and is, a relevant one: relevant when I met the families and priests of Rio de Janeiro, relevant in the meeting with men and women religious in São Paolo, and relevant in contact with the labor world, with the workers, at São Paolo. Here, however, at this meeting with you, the question seems to me particularly relevant. To a large extent, in fact, the future of the Church in this great, beautiful, and promising Brazilian nation depends on you. In this, the pilgrim People of God, and men in general, feel challenged and want someone to point out goals to them and the way to answer correctly the question: "Where are you going?"

And you, are you not, or do you not want to be, this someone?

Vocation—a Mystery That Man Accepts

My first message is for you, beloved young people, for you who keep the special call of Christ in your hearts as a powerful impulse. Always be aware of the predilection that this initiative of the Divine Master signifies for you: every vocation is part of a great divine plan, in which each of those called is very important. Christ Himself, the Word of God, the "Called" par excellence, "did not exalt himself to be made a high priest, but was appointed by him who said to him, 'You are my Son, today I have begotten you' (Ps. 2:7); as he says also in another place, 'You are a priest for ever, after the order of Melchizedek' (Ps. 110:4)" (Heb. 5:5).

Vocation is, therefore, a mystery that man accepts and lives in the depths of his being. A gift and a grace, it depends on supreme divine freedom, and in its total reality, it escapes our understanding. We cannot demand explanations from the Giver of all goods—"Why have you made me thus?" (Rom. 9:20) because He who calls is also "He who is" (cf. Ex. 3:14).

The vocation of each one merges, up to a certain point, with his very being: it can be said that vocation and person become just one thing. This means that in God's creative initiative there enters a particular act of love for those called not only to salvation, but also to the ministry of salvation. Therefore, from all eternity, since we began to exist in the plans of the Creator, and He willed us to be creatures, He also willed us to be "called," preparing in us the gifts and conditions for the personal, conscious, and opportune response to the call of Christ and of the Church. God who loves us, who is love, is also "He who calls" (cf. Rom. 9:11).

Therefore, in the presence of a vocation we adore the mystery; we respond lovingly to the initiative of love, we say "yes" to the call.

Do Not Harden Your Hearts

However, you well know that at the origin of every vocation there is always Jesus, the supreme incarnation of the Love of God; in Christ's love vocation finds its *raison d'etre.* He Himself explained it: "You did not choose me, but I chose you and appointed you that you should go and bear fruit..." (Jn. 15:16). Let me repeat what I wrote recently, as if said for you alone: "I, the Pope, am the humble and zealous servant of that same love by which Christ was moved, when He called the disciples to follow Him" (Message for the World Day of Prayer for Vocations, 1980, no. 4).

Fundamentally, He who calls us is the Father, the vinedresser (Jn. 15:1), and He draws us to the One whom He sent (cf. Jn. 6:44). His call continues in us the work of love that began in creation. But it is always Christ—directly or by means of His "universal sacrament of salvation" which is the Church—who enables us to perceive the divine call to a work which is personal cooperation with Him. He did so with the first Apostles: "He called to him those whom he desired; and they came to him" (Mk. 3:13; cf. 6:7).

The response depends on the generosity of the heart of the one called, because He who calls always leaves freedom of choice: "If you would..." (cf. Mt. 19:21). At this meeting with you, full of gratitude I raise my spirit to God who loves us always and gives us comfort and hope (cf. 2 Thes. 2:16), and I implore that "your love may abound more and more, with knowledge and all discernment, that you may approve what is excellent" (Phil. 1:9-10). Do not let yourselves be troubled like the young man in the Gospel. It is worth exchanging "great possessions" for "a treasure in heaven."

At this point I cannot but call upon each of you in particular, in an urgent way, as I am accustomed in similar circumstances to call upon youths who have the same ideal: listen to the Lord, the great Friend. He looks you in the eye and He speaks to your heart, in the intimacy of personal prayer (cf. Rev. 3:20), of communal prayer (cf. Mt. 18:20), and of the liturgy, because He "is always present in His Church, especially in her liturgical celebrations" (Const. *Sacrosanctum Concilium*, no. 7). Rest assured that He will enlighten you and help you to discover and love the meaning and the value of vocation. Who knows whether today, at this meeting "in His name," He will not tell you some of His secrets? If this be so, "do not harden your hearts" (Heb. 3:8). Only in openness to God's voice will you be able to find the joy of complete self-fulfillment.

Priestly and Religious Formation

Beside you, as ministers of Christ and interpreters of His internal aspirations, are those to whom the Church has entrusted the delicate task of your formation. Turning my attention to them, I am happy to recall in the first place the long tradition of commitment for priestly formation in Brazil, with some characteristics recognized by everyone. It goes back to the first experiences in the Colleges of Bahia, Sao Paolo, and Rio de Janeiro; it passes through the period formerly designated as "the Age of Convents," and through alternate times of trial and prosperity, until it reaches the first ecclesiastical organization. In the 18th century there appear seminaries properly so-called, among which those of Mariana, Olinda, and Caraca, to name a few, have left a mark in the history of Brazil.

At this point how could I fail to recognize the merits and appreciate the important role of the orders and religious congregations?

Subsequently, with seminaries such as were recommended by the Council of Trent, established in many parts of the immense territory, there continued the formation of successive generations of priests, some of whom, in this last century, came to Rome to complete their studies and formation, first at the Latin American College, then in the Brazilian College, or in the Roman houses of religious institutes, valuable means to maintain the traditional ties between Catholic Brazil and St. Peter's See, in the communion of the universal Church.

Before these glorious traditions of the past, a question imposes itself on the heart of the Pope, worried by the *sollicitudo omnium ecclesiarum* (2 Cor. 11:28): in a decisive moment for its destiny and for that of the world, such as the present, will Brazil have the seminaries, religious houses, or other ecclesiastical institutes; will it have, above all, the rectors and teachers capable of preparing priests and religious who will be equal to the problems raised by a continually growing population, with increasingly vast and complex pastoral needs?

The question involves a fundamental point of ecclesial life. I would like to pause for a few moments to speak about it to you who have, in various capacities, responsibility for the seminaries and houses of formation. The centuries-old experience and the considered reflection of the Church prove the absolute necessity of these structures for the preparation of priests and religious. The Second Vatican Council has confirmed that the way followed by the Church through the centuries is the right one, and that it must not, therefore, be abandoned.

The formation of a priest and of a religious cannot be left to improvization. It is God's grace that inspires vocation, it is God's grace that creates the priest and the religious. But this grace is given in the Church and for the Church: so it is up to the Church to test the authenticity of a call and guide its development up to the goal of Holy Orders and religious vows. Now for the Church, on the basis of her tradition and experience, all this cannot be fully carried out without an institution called by a highly significant name: the seminary, and other similar institutions for religious formation.

Certainly, the seminary and other educational institutions need to be updated. The Church knows this. It is one of her constant concerns. The Church knows that reality changes according to times and places; she reflects on reality and follows reality, which bears within it the signs of divine Providence. Therefore, she proposes precise norms, and in this way tries to help those responsible for priestly and religious formation in their difficult work, which to be efficacious must always be carried out in the Church, with the Church, and for the Church.

For this reason my venerated Predecessors have taken care, with admirable solicitude, to deal with the subjects of priestly and religious formation, such as modern pastoral needs required. For the same reason the Holy See has not failed to recall, comment on, and explain the requirements pointed out by the Council through a series of documents, in which those responsible for priestly and religious formation must see a renewed testimony of trust, understanding, and love.

As I speak to you, I have in mind the difficulties which disturb the modern world and which have repercussions in the life and the Church. Seminaries and other institutions of formation could hardly be spared. The very proposal of priestly and religious life has quite often found obstacles even in those who should have proclaimed it courageously or might have accepted it generously.

Even if the difficulties were greater than those we know, our sacred duty remains that of evangelizing the People of God with regard to the divine dignity of the ministerial priesthood and of the lofty ideal of consecrated life. For this reason, beloved priests and religious, I call upon you to meditate again on the Constitution *Lumen gentium* and the Decrees *Presbyterorum ordinis* and *Perfectae caritatis* of the Second Vatican Council. In particular, I call upon you to reread the letter I addressed to all the priests in the Church on the occasion of Holy Thursday, 1979, to reaffirm the sacred doctrine of the Church on the ministerial priesthood, which is participation in the priesthood of Christ by means of Holy Orders, and the gift of Christ to His and our community (cf. nos. 3 and 4).

If we are deeply convinced of this truth, if we communicate it in its entirety to the People of God, if we bear witness to it with our lives, then the difficulties of our times will not frighten us.

Balance and Courage Are Necessary

Having reaffirmed these fundamental principles which spring from faith, allow me to mention some practical aspects which deserve prudent consideration for the good of the Church and of priestly and religious life.

The Church wishes the most adequate means and methods to be sought for the formation of the priest and religious of today. The directives of the Council and the subsequent ones of the Holy See are all aimed in this direction. The Council rightly suggested dividing seminary communities that are too large. It proposed that aspirants to the priesthood keep in touch with the community and offer assistance for pastoral activity in the places their formation took place. There can be no doubt about the pedagogical value of these guidelines.

However, after a sufficient period of experimentation, we all have the duty to re-examine some initiatives, undertaken certainly with good intentions, but which may distort the directives of the Council and lead to disappointing and harmful results. What things must be corrected or completed, for example, in the various undertakings, not always happy ones, aimed at replacing seminaries, especially by means of the so-called "little communities"? What are the pros and cons of a formation of future priests exclusively within the communities in which they will subsequently have to carry out their ministry? How to avoid reducing to a minimum the program of studies and of the seminary curriculum to the evident detriment of the specific intellectual and spiritual formation which belongs to the new minister of God?

Balance and courage are necessary, especially on the part of the bishops, to direct clearly all the points concerning the formation of new ministers, especially priests. We rejoice to see that the far-sighted norms of the Second Vatican Council are again taken into due consideration, accepted, and put into practice, while experiments which have not yielded fruit, or have turned out to be negative, are reshaped, made relevant, and, when necessary, abandoned.

But above all, I am anxious to stress that in this task, the work of priests and religious remains fundamental, be they superiors, teachers, or masters of novices. Your mission is a marvelous but difficult one. The pastors of dioceses and those responsible for religious life have reflected and prayed before choosing you and entrusting to you one of the most delicate ministries that exist in the Church: to form those who will form the People of God.

Having accepted this mission, you must feel responsible for your personal preparation. The Council stressed this point (cf. *Optatam totius,* no. 5). The First Synod of Bishops gave precise guidelines. Your bishops and religious superiors will help you. But your continual improvement on the spiritual, intellectual, and pastoral levels depends on you, on awareness of your duty.

Your spirituality must draw from the pure spring that is Christ, the Teacher of teachers, Pastor of our souls, the supreme Model of all educators and of all education. Your intellectual preparation must always be updated, in total fidelity to the Magisterium and to the living Tradition of the Church, in humble and affectionate acceptance of the Word of God which surpasses all human wisdom. Your pastoral efficiency cannot but increase with integration in the diocesan presbyterium, which experience enriches you, and which you enrich with your experience.

With this complete preparation your mission will be carried out laboriously, but also joyfully, under the blessing of God who does not leave without help anyone who offers Him his unconditional cooperation. Thus prepared, you will find light and strength to carry out a work of authentic evangelical pedagogy.

You will guide the aspirants entrusted to you to achieve the height of spirituality, that height which will then sustain them in the labors of apostolic ministry and in fidelity to the commitments assumed on behalf of the Church. You will guide them to discern their vocation clearly, to strengthen their character, to accept the sacrifice of a life dedicated wholly to God and to the Church. You will guide them to acquire a solid, healthy, and open education, which is required today of anyone who is to be in his turn a teacher of the People of God. You will guide them towards pastoral knowledge and wisdom, which is the proclamation of the Word of God, the celebration of the divine Mysteries, spiritual care for the community and for individual souls. In a word: your disciples will draw upon your riches, as you draw on the inexhaustible riches of Christ's heart.

Shoulder Your Responsibilities

This is, beloved sons, the exhortation that wells up from my heart; this is the instruction I wish to entrust to each of you: put your mind, your heart, your energies generously at the disposal of Christ. I say it to you, superiors and educators, who in daily dedication to your delicate task, are called to be a sign and instrument of the service of Christ who is building up His body. I say it to you, young people, who have accepted the call and have agreed to set out in the footsteps of Christ, in order to be tomorrow the witnesses to His love among your brothers.

But my thought and my exhortation turn also to Christian families, which the Second Vatican Council indicated as the "first seminary" of vocation (cf. Decree *Optatam totius*, no. 2). It is up to them to create in the home that climate of faith, charity, and prayer that will guide their children to assume an attitude of generous availability for God's initiative and His plan for the world. Alongside the family, the school has an important role. Teachers, especially if they are Catholic, must feel the commitment not only to enrich the minds of their pupils with the contents of culture, but also to make their spirits sensitive to the call of moral values and to the stirring attraction of great ideals.

A special word for the parish, whose contribution is decisive in this connection. There, in fact, the young live their Christian experience; there they listen to the proclamation of the Word of God and take part in the celebration of the signs of salvation; there, moreover, they encounter the witness of the various vocations and the various ministries. The importance of associations, groups, and ecclesial movements is therefore evident, not to mention the person of the priests in charge of the pastoral care of the community, as the normal instrument of God's call to more generous service for the coming of the kingdom. I exhort all members of the Christian community, therefore, to shoulder their respective responsibilities in this essential area of ecclesial life.

Christ needs the contribution of all to bring to other hearts the word that "not all men can receive" (cf. Mt. 19:11), that is, the word of the call to unreserved surrender to the cause of the kingdom.

Repeating to everyone the expression of my gratitude, my trust, and my affection, I entrust your intentions and your resolutions to the Blessed Virgin Aparecida. In particular I ask her to take you, young people, under her motherly protection in this decisive period of your lives, and to lead you with a firm hand to the encounter with Christ, who loves you, who calls you, who waits for you, who will be your joy today and always.

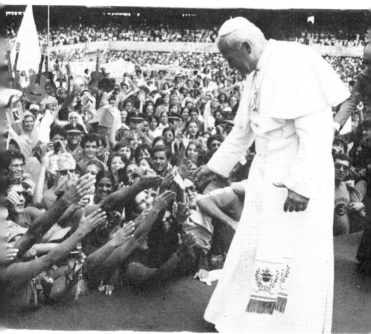

I Entrust You to Mary, Our Hope

In the afternoon of July 5, 1980, the Pope met with immigrants and the descendents of immigrants at Curitiba, Brazil. The following are the Holy Father's words to the young people present for the occasion.

With a particularly warm appeal I address the younger generation, you children and young people. Take this heritage won and paid for with the toil, the work, the sacrifice, and the prayer of your ancestors. Take it and develop it. Work for the glory of God, for your own good, for the good of the society and the country in which you live, for the good of the Church in this country. God is with you, the Church is with you, and in conformity with the mission entrusted to her by Christ, she will try to meet your needs. The Pope is with you.

As a memento of this historic meeting today, I leave you a copy of the image of Our Lady of Czestochowa. I know that you are preparing for a pilgrimage to this image. The Mother of Christ and Mother of every man, she who stood beside the cross when her Son was dying on it, she who was assiduous in prayer together with the Apostles in the upper room when the Holy Spirit descended on them as the fruit of redemption, will, by means of this image of the Bright Mountain, as she has done for years in Poland, visit your parishes, churches, chapels, environments, families and homes, your fields marked by the cross, which are the ground and the proofs of hard work, often exceeding human strength, of sacrifice, suffering, nostalgia, dedication, faith, the prayer of your ancestors, and your everyday toil.

So to her, the Mother of the Redeemer and the Mother of our hope, I entrust you all: priests, sisters, fathers and mothers of families, children, the young, the sick, those who live in loneliness, the abandoned, the aged, the suffering. Those who work in the fields, in factories, in universities, in schools, in offices. All together and each one individually, you who are present here and all those united with us spiritually. I entrust to her your present and your future, your faith, hope, and charity. Your work, joys, concerns and worries. I entrust to her in a special way the young generation and their future.

Open Witness
to the Faith

At the conclusion of the general audience on July 23, 1980, the Pope addressed the young people as follows.

I now address a particularly affectionate greeting to the young, who with their exuberant enthusiasm, crowd and bring joy to this square of St. Peter's.

I thank you, dear young people, for your presence. If I welcome you with special affection, it is because I really have confidence in you, because, in my experience among the young, formerly as a lecturer in a university and in my preceding meetings with them in cultural clubs and in excursions in the mountains, I have become convinced that you yourselves, young people, are one of the significant ways of the Church, because you bear an open witness to faith, with sincere commitment and nobility of ideals, thus glorifying the Redeemer of man, Jesus our Brother and our true Friend.

With these sentiments I wish you a serene summer rest and I willingly bless you.

Choose the Better Portion

On July 24, 1980, the Holy Father celebrated Holy Mass in the gardens of the Pontifical Villa of Castel Gandolfo for the young people of the international movement "OASIS," gathered at Rocca di Papa on the occasion of the thirtieth anniversary of its institution.

At the Liturgy of the Word, the Pope delivered the following homily to the eight hundred or so young people present.

Beloved brothers and sons belonging to the "OASIS" movement!

Taking part in the international congress on the occasion of the thirtieth anniversary of the foundation of your association, you wished to conclude it with holy Mass celebrated by the Pope. It is really a great joy for me to meet you on this occasion which is the culmination of your meeting, and I extend my most affectionate greeting to your leaders and to all of you. And I say thank you for your ardent and fervent youth, for your generosity, and for the joy you bring to me, to the Church, and to the world!

Thirty years have passed since that day, during the 1950 Holy Year, in which this ecclesial movement, such an important and decisive one, came into being humbly and without notice. It was called "OASIS" because you wished to indicate—as Pius XII, of venerated memory, stressed— that "in the desert of this world, so arid because it is so parched" it was your desire and deliberate will that the life of God should be born, grow, and multiply, with you as channels supplied by Him who is the source of living water (cf. *Address* on November 23, 1952).

Since then the little seed has developed into a large tree, with its fruitful branches spreading into thirty-five states on all continents, grouping thousands and thousands of young people who let themselves be guided completely and joyfully by love of Christ in order to bear witness to Him in modern society. For this spiritual phenomenon, such a significant and effective one, we first of all thank the Lord and the Blessed Virgin, to whom you are particularly consecrated; then we also express our gratitude to those who confidently started it and have continued it with persevering dedication.

A Hidden Leaven in Society

Today, however, after the celebration of the thirtieth anniversary, when you are preparing to return as hidden but priceless leaven to a society which is in such need of certainty and salvation, you are expecting from the Vicar of Christ a motto which will commit you further in your "consecration," so beautiful and so necessary.

Referring to the word "OASIS," which immediately suggests the idea of peace, rest, and serenity, I wish to recall the meeting of Christ with Martha and Mary, which took place in Bethany, which was in a way Jesus' "oasis," as we read in the Gospel last Sunday.

The evangelist writes that Jesus was received by Martha into her house: "She had a sister called Mary, who sat at the Lord's feet and listened to his teaching. But Martha was distracted with much serving; and she went to him and said, 'Lord, do you not care that my sister has left me to serve alone? Tell her then to help me.' But the Lord answered her, 'Martha, Martha, you are anxious and troubled about many things; one thing is needful. Mary has chosen the good portion, which shall not be taken away from her' " (Lk. 10:38-42). Evidently, Jesus was not reproaching Martha for her solicitude about household tasks, full of thoughtfulness and kindness, but for her excessive concern with material things, which almost made her forget the "absolute precedence" due to the divine Guest; while He praised Mary, who in listening to Jesus had chosen the good portion.

For the "good portion" is here: in listening to the word of God, in listening to the message of Christ! And it is precisely here that the spirit of "OASIS" lies! You wish to choose the "good portion," listening to the word of God and remaining faithful witnesses to His message of salvation.

This is, in fact, the only thing that we really need: the light of revelation and the redeeming power of grace. Without the light of Christ, everything becomes enigmatic, obscure, contradictory, even absurd, as is unfortunately confirmed by so many movements of contemporary agnosticism. And the frantic agitation of the multitudes becomes a tragic and frightening reality, if the certainty that comes solely from Christ the Savior is lacking. "Jesus Christ is the Lord"—I said recently to the crowd at Curitiba—"He is the only orientation of the spirit, the only direction of the intelligence, the will, and the heart for all of us; He is the Redeemer of man; He is the Redeemer of the world; in Him lies our salvation."

You, in "OASIS," who, listening to the Word of God wish to choose the good portion, remain faithful to it, therefore, and bear witness to it, in every place, in a spirit of service and love!

—From the word of Jesus we learn, first and foremost, the very nature of God, who is Life, Light, Love, Trinity. No philosopher and theologian can penetrate the essence of God; only Jesus, the Word Incarnate, can reveal and guarantee this fundamental truth. And because of this we are certain that there is a relationship of love between God the Creator and Man: every human being is an eternal heartbeat of God's love;

—from the word of Jesus we know our eternal destiny: only Jesus, with His divine word, can assure us absolutely concerning the immortality of the soul and the final resurrection of the body, as a result of which it is worthwhile being born, living, and projecting our existence beyond time towards endless happiness;

—from the word of Jesus we learn, furthermore, where the true dignity of man lies, namely, in participation in divine life itself by means of grace. "If a man loves me, he will keep my word, and my Father will love him, and we will come to him and make our home with him" (Jn. 14:23). True joy, real greatness, supreme dignity, are found only in the life of grace;

—from the word of Jesus we learn how we must behave, because He reveals to us that the will of God is expressed in the moral law and in the supreme commandment of mutual charity. The will of God, in fact, is the absolute determinant between good and evil, the guideline for correct behavior and for true pedagogy;

—finally, from the word of Jesus we know also His presence, always current and alive in time and in history, by means of the Church, willed and founded by Him, which gives us certainty about the truths to believe and to practice, and offers us the Eucharist, a mystery of faith and at the same time a supreme manifestation of love.

Have the Courage of Truth

This is the "good portion" which you want to choose by listening to Jesus; these are the riches that you must possess! Certainly, as St. Paul wrote to the Corinthians, "we have this treasure in earthen vessels," that is, we are frail and weak; but all this happens "to show that the transcendent power belongs to God and not to us" (2 Cor. 4:7). So always have the courage of truth, firmness, and faithfulness to the spirit of "OASIS."

This is the marvelous program which you must carry out day by day; this is your service of love, mindful of what the Divine Master said to the Apostles: "...whoever would be great among you must be your servant,...even as the Son of man came not to be served but to serve, and to give his life as a ransom for many" (Mt. 20:26-28).

Beloved young people of "OASIS!" The world needs your faith, your purity, your joy, your help, your smile. You too, who have chosen "the good portion," must be evangelizers. I entrust you to the Blessed Virgin, with tender affection and great confidence, and with you I repeat the invocation which I addressed to you during my apostolic journey in Brazil: "Mother, wrapped in the mystery of your Son, often without being able to understand, but capable of keeping everything and pondering it in your heart, make us evangelizers always understand that beyond techniques and strategies, preparations and plans, to evangelize is to immerse oneself in the mystery of Christ and try to communicate something of Him to one's brothers" (Homily of the holy Mass at Belém).

With these wishes I impart from the bottom of my heart the conciliatory apostolic blessing, a pledge of abundant heavenly favors, which I gladly extend to all members and friends of the "OASIS" groups in the world!

Dear French-speaking young people, I myself was very happy at this meeting with your "OASIS" movement. I congratulate you! I encourage you to deepen your union with Christ, listening to His word and in prayer: it is He who makes you His home and who then gives you serenity in faith. Be on your part witnesses to His peace, and to His pure and strong love, among all those that God puts on your path.

I greet you also in English. Remember that it is only Jesus who can satisfy our spiritual thirst. The water that Jesus gives becomes within us a spring of water welling up to eternal life. Drink of this water yourselves and provide it for those who, like the Samaritan woman, say: "Give me this water, that I may not thirst."

A special very cordial greeting to all the young people coming from the various Spanish-speaking nations.

Be courageous on the way to Christ, who will make you discover this magnificent oasis of peace, grace, and superior ideals that give your existence a new dimension. And commit yourselves generously to the task of showing to those who are younger that life is worth living, by illuminating it always with the great values of brotherhood and the true love that Christ teaches us. May Mary, our Mother, accompany you on your course.

Dear Portuguese-speaking brothers,

Greeting you cordially, I wish this Eucharist and meeting of brothers to keep the spirit of the "OASIS" movement alive: in the light of the Blessed Virgin, cultivate splendid divine grace; be "leaven in the dough" in which you are called to live and keep your eyes and heart fixed on the Lord Jesus, to bear witness to the destiny, dignity, and true values of human persons; and always serve the cause of man with your fidelity to God and to yourselves, in the light of the mystery of Christ the Redeemer, with optimism, serenity, and joy.

Bear Jesus in Your Heart

On July 30, 1980, the Holy Father spoke a special word to the young people present at the general audience.

My thought and my greeting now turn to you, young people present here, who come from all over the world in this period of rest from your normal commitments of study. Seeing people and cities, you will have the possibility of enriching your knowledge; but always try to keep intact the freshness of your youth and the staunchness of your Christian faith, lived in continual joy, which comes from deep friendship with Christ.

I address a special greeting to you, leaders and members of the youth movement of the "Pontifical Mission Aid Societies," who are celebrating in Rome these days your congress on the subject: "Mission—Vocation—Catechesis," and I hope that you will always bear in your heart and spread especially among those of your own age the ardor and commitment of personal witness to the message of Jesus.

May my apostolic blessing strengthen these wishes.

Let Your Actions Reflect Your Soul

The Holy Father addressed a special greeting to young people present at the general audience of August 6, 1980, as follows.

You have come to this audience in large numbers from various localities, dear young people, and I thank you for your participation. Today the liturgy celebrates a mysterious and consoling episode of the life of Jesus: the Transfiguration of His corporeal aspect, invested with the glory of the Father, on Mount Tabor. In connection with that fact, I wish to repeat to you a sentence of my message to the young people of Paris: "Have very great respect for your body and for the bodies of others! Let your body be in the service of your inner self! Let your gestures, your looks, always be the reflection of your soul! Worship of the body? No, never! Contempt for the body? Again, no! Control of the body? Yes! Transfiguration of the body? Even more!" (June 1, 1980) This I wish you with affection. May my fatherly blessing help you.

Overcome Evil with Love

On the evening of August 12, 1980, the Holy Father received two groups of visitors at Castel Gandolfo: a large representation from the Community of Nomadelphia and numerous young people belonging to the "Giorgio La Pira" Youth Organization of Florence.

After a performance of dances characteristic of the Nomadelphians, and after the showing of a film on the history of the community, the Holy Father addressed the following to all those present.

At the conclusion of such a beautiful evening I wish to express my kindest thanks.

You have so much wanted this particular meeting with the Pope; but I, too, am very happy to have had you here with me, to have seen you, to have met and listened to you, and to have been able to think of you as dear friends.

First of all, I want to thank the members of the "Giorgio La Pira" Youth Workers Group from Florence, who are engaged in a special way in the Christian formation of young people in the diocese of Tuscany, with a particularly ecumenical goal and with the typical experiences of "communities" by means of school summer camps. I know that in November last year, your dear Archbishop led a numerous group of your organization to London, for a meeting with the youth of the Anglican Church. Consequently, I express to you my complete satisfaction with your activities of cultural formation and refinement for the good of the diocese and the parishes.

I also thank Don Zeno and his community of Nomadelphia! Who does not know Don Zeno and his various hardships in founding "Nomadelphia" and trying an experiment in human and Christian life where the law is solely and totally brotherhood and charity? This we know for certain: that since this experiment began, four thousand abandoned children have found a family home. And thank you also for the performance you have given in the Pope's presence, after having given enjoyment to many communities and towns. Your joy, your sincere and keen enthusiasm are a great comfort to me.

And now, before I leave you, what can I say to you, if not "persevere"? Yes, my dear ones, carry on with joy and zeal to accomplish God's will. One speaks at this time about a return to religion, about a nostalgia for the authentic and eternal values, about a need for real and sure certainties which give a meaning to life and a significance to one's own choices. This is certainly a very beautiful and comforting reality, which must lead us to the definitive acceptance of God's will as the only true salvation of man.

Knowledge of Christ

Well then, you show what God wants from man by living your lives in a real and practical way:

—God certainly wants the knowledge of Christ, who took on flesh and became part of our history as man. "This is eternal life"—Jesus said—"that they know you, the only true God, and Jesus Christ whom you have sent" (Jn. 17:3). And St. John wrote: "God has sent his only begotten Son into the world so that we may have life in him.... We ourselves have seen and witnessed that the Father has sent his Son as savior of the world. Whoever recognizes that Jesus is the Son of God, God lives in him and he in God" (1 Jn. 4:9, 14-15). But where can we find today the authentic Christ, His certain word, His ways of grace and salvation? Only the Apostles, and thus their successors, that is, the Church, can guarantee the certain faith in Jesus, by divine mandate. Therefore, continue to get to know Jesus more and more, and better and better, in the doctrinal and disciplinary faith of the Church, which wants only the well-being and the salvation of humanity.

God Wants Charity

—God certainly wants charity; it is the "new commandment" left by Jesus to His followers: "Love one another as I have loved you" (Jn. 13:34). Persevere, therefore, in charity! It is a new command which asks us continually to love others as Jesus loved us! Let's go on then, with courage and conviction! There is a whole world to help, to welcome, to comfort! A Christian's preoccupation must be charity: we will be judged on charity shown towards our fellowmen. The fatal discord of violence, hate, cruelty, and selfishness must be overcome by the good seed of our love.

Dearest ones,

While we are preparing ourselves for the solemnity of Holy Mary's Assumption into heaven, I entrust to her your intentions of perseverance! Mary, who is our Mother, points out to us the goal of heaven towards which we are aiming, day by day. Pray to her with deep devotion: her tender love has the wonderful power to transform the painful mysteries, which sometimes sadden our lives, into joyful mysteries transfigured by love. I grant now to all of you my affectionate and conciliatory blessing.

Mary Raises Our Minds to Heaven

During the general audience on August 20, 1980, the Holy Father addressed the young people present with the following words.

I say hello now to you, young people, among whom there are 350 volunteers from the Home and Hearth Movement, coming from various nations of the five continents, gathered at the "Marianopoli Center" at Rocca di Papa for the annual course in study and spirituality.

Dearest ones, while I thank you heartily for your presence here, I call your attention to the imminent feast of our Lady assumed into heaven. We know the Mary Immaculate, Spouse of the Holy Spirit, Mother of Christ and the Church, first of the redeemed, at the end of her life on earth was raised in spirit and body to heavenly glory. Such an admirable event teaches that man's destiny is not consumed with time, but is projected and completed in heaven, beside God.

May the message of faith and Christian hope, deriving from the imminent Marian celebration, reecho always in your hearts.

Christ Believes in Youth

On August 28, 1980, the Holy Father concelebrated Mass in English at Castel Gandolfo for a large pilgrimage of the Catholic Youth Council from the Archdiocese of Dublin. Among the concelebrants were the Most Reverend Dermot Ryan, Archbishop of Dublin, and his Auxiliary Bishop, Most Reverend Laurence Forristal. The Holy Father delivered the following homily.

Dear young people of Dublin,

The love of Christ has gathered us together this morning! Nothing else can adequately explain our marvelous unity. We have come together in the name of Jesus, and He is present with us. Jesus Christ is in our midst (cf. Mt. 18:20).

You have come to Rome as representatives of the youth of Dublin; you have wished to return the visit that I made to you in Ireland. At the same time you are giving me another opportunity to speak to you about Christ, to remind you of your Christian dignity, and to proclaim to you a fellowship that the Holy Spirit has given to all of us: a fellowship with the Father and with His Son Jesus Christ (cf. 1 Jn. 1:3).

You have come here, moreover, so that all of us together may celebrate our life in Christ, and through the merits of His redemption find ever greater communion with the Most Holy Trinity. A wonderful aspect of our Eucharist is that, in it, we bring to Christ the fabric of our daily lives. He accepts our offering, unites it to His own oblation, and presents it to His eternal Father. At the same time, in the Mass, we listen to God's word as proclaimed by the Church—a proclamation that reaches its highest expression in the very renewal of Christ's sacrifice. As we celebrate this Eucharistic Sacrifice we are performing an action that is at the very summit of our Christian lives; here our Christian dignity is realized to the full. And all of this is something that we are doing together as a community, a community in Christ and with Christ, as members of His Body, members of His holy Church.

And from this Eucharistic Celebration you will go out to fulfill your calling, the activities of your life, and finally your destiny. For a few moments, therefore, let us reflect, within this sacred context of God's word, on these important elements of the Christian life.

To Do, To Love and To Serve More

Each one of you is individually called by Christ, called to be part of His kingdom and to play a role in His mission of salvation. These are the great realities of your Confirmation. Having called you by name, God sends you forth to accomplish what He wants you to do. He says to each of you what He said to Jeremiah the Prophet: "I am with you to protect you." He seals His protection over you by putting His words into your mouth. In the expression of the Psalmist, the Word of God becomes for you a lamp for your feet and a light for your path (cf. Ps. 119:105). Christ calls you to lead a new life based on the beatitudes, with new criteria of judgment, a fresh spiritual outlook and a transformed pattern of life. Incorporated into the newness of Christ's own life, only a constant turning to Him will give you fulfillment and joy. A repeated conversion of heart becomes the condition for the usefulness of your activities and for the attainment of your destiny.

As you pursue your fundamental Christian calling, you will be summoned to perform joyfully and faithfully the activities of each moment, each day, each week. For most of you, the field of your activities is the secular world itself in need of the Gospel leaven. Your task is crystal clear: to bring Christ to the world and to bring the world to Christ. I am sure that you have already grasped all of this. Is this not the context of your motto: "To do more, to love more, to serve more"?

This "doing," this "loving," this "serving" must be expressed in many ways. You are called, for instance, to be men and women of honesty and integrity: "to live in truth and love" according to the petition of this morning's Mass. You are called to open your hearts to the justice of the Gospel, so that in turn you may be instruments of justice and builders of peace.

You are young and you are rightfully looking for understanding from your elders, your priests, your beloved parents, all who make up the preceding generations of society—and you are hoping for the compassion of friendship. But precisely because you are young with the vitality of Christ's grace and share enthusiasm for His message, you know that there is something even higher and more noble; hence it becomes possible for you to pray "not so much to be understood, as to understand; to be loved as to love." And so you are called to be leaders of the next generation through understanding and love. Dear young people: Is not almost half of your archdiocese made up of young people under twenty-one? Can you have any doubt but that the future of Dublin and the rest of Ireland really does depend on your generosity, your commitment to Christ and your service to your brothers and sisters?

You are called to understand each other, to work together, to walk together the path of life—together with each other and with Christ—to respect humanity in everyone, even in those who have lost a sense of their own dignity. You must find Christ in others and give Christ to others—the Christ who alone is the hope of the world! In all the circumstances of your lives you are called to be bearers of a message of hope, called to be ready, in the words of St. Peter, with an answer for anyone who asks you "to account for the hope that is in you" (1 Pt. 3:15).

With this hope, with understanding and love, equipped with all the principles of your Catholic Faith, you will be able to face serenely the issues of daily living. And you can be sure that Mary, Mother of Jesus and bright "Sun of the Irish race" will always assist you by her intercession.

Complicated social and economic problems are not subject to facile solution. Nevertheless, a perseverance born of hope and a fraternal commitment to the needs of one's brothers and sisters are indispensable conditions for real progress in these fields. Your Christian calling urges you to make your contribution—great or small, but always unique and irreplaceable—to building up a just and peaceful society. And this same Christian calling invites you, individually and all together, to help—through prayer, sacrifice, personal Christian discipline and a number of ways open to your own creative initiative—to bring the Gospel of salvation into the lives of many people. The parish needs you and your contribution of Christian living. The community needs your vitality, your joy, your efforts at working together for the good of all. Even the Creator Himself has asked for your cooperation in sustaining His creation. Be convinced always that your daily work has great value in the eyes of God. Make every effort to ensure that its quality is worthy of Christ and His members. And remember, too, that Christ wants to accept the gift of your work and of your lives, and offer them to His Father. In fact, He is doing this right now, in this Eucharist.

I have already mentioned the need to turn constantly to Christ and to be ever newly converted to Him. Christian living is not complete without this renewed conversion, and conversion is not fully authentic without the sacrament of Penance. Dear young people of Dublin: Christ wants to come to meet you regularly, frequently, in a personal way, in a personal encounter of loving mercy, forgiveness and healing. He wants to sustain you in your weakness and keep lifting you up, drawing you closer to His heart. As I explained in my Encyclical *Redemptor hominis,* the encounter of this sacrament is a right that belongs to Christ and to each of you (cf. no. 20). And so the Pope is very much in earnest when he now exhorts you: Do not deprive Christ of His right in this sacrament, and never surrender your own.

Dependence on God's Grace

And finally, dear young people, from this Eucharist you will go out to fulfill your destiny. This fulfillment depends on God's grace—as the feast of St. Augustine so forcefully recalls to us today. But it also requires the assent of your free will. You must repeatedly say yes to Christ, in order to ensure the success of your unique part in God's plan for the salvation of the world. Here we must reflect again on the importance of fidelity to your calling. I have mentioned on other occasions how much the course of history has been shaped in Ireland and throughout the world by the fidelity of one man—the fidelity of St. Patrick. The proportion may be different, but the principle is the same: Christ has a special work for each one of you, a work that only you can do. Without your cooperation it would remain undone. Christ directs each of you, in a personal way, towards a destiny, for the attainment of which we are interdependent. Look to Him today—look to Christ. Accept His offer as He extends His hand to you, embraces you with the strength of His arm, and reveals to you the love of His Sacred Heart.

And now, in conclusion, let me add just one more word. When I was in Galway, I told all those present there that I believe in youth with all my heart, that I believe in the youth of Ireland, every one of you. And today I would like to add something to that message, and it is this: Because of what Christ has given you, because of His own free gifts of life and grace, He believes in you. Christ believes in youth, the youth of Ireland, every one of you. And He loves you. Young people of Dublin, Christ loves you! Christ loves you and wants to love through you! Amen.

"Be Courageous!"

On August 30, 1980, in front of the sanctuary dedicated to Our Lady of the Cross, the Holy Father met with several thousands of young people, particularly Abruzzesi and foreign students of the University of Aquila. After hearing welcoming addresses by two of the students, the Holy Father delivered the following message.

Beloved young people of Aquila, Abruzzi and Molise!

I tell you first of all my great joy in meeting you at this famous sanctuary dedicated to the Blessed Virgin!

You prepared for the Pope's visit by going along the "Via Mariana" this morning, a monument of faith and piety which Cardinal Carlo Confalonieri had built here when he was Archbishop of Aquila, and stopping at the fifteen respective shrines, you meditated on the mysteries of the rosary.

I heartily thank you for this spiritual initiative, as well as for your presence, so devoted, joyful, and numerous; I greet you all with particular affection. I also intend at this moment to extend my grateful and brotherly greeting to the Cardinal Dean, Cardinal Corrado Bafile, a son of this city, and to all the bishops of the Episcopal Conference of Abruzzi, who have wished to be present with you at this significant meeting.

I have come to your land to honor in a special way Saint Bernardine of Siena, on the 6th centenary of his birth. I have come to see you, too, dear young people, to speak to you, to hear you, to establish a more cordial and concrete friendship with you, to look you in the eye, as Jesus did, to leave you a message that will be for you a powerful reminder and a designed commitment.

And you have come to meet the Pope with your joy, your goodness, your liveliness, and also with your anxieties, your questions. You have come to listen to his voice and pray with him! I thank you again for this kindness and availability of yours.

The Value of Knowledge of Jesus

Reflecting now for a moment with you on the figure of St. Bernardine, I wish to propose to you some directions which can serve you as a program of life, following in the steps of the great saint.

Learn first of all from St. Bernardine the essential and determinant value of knowledge of Jesus.

You know the life of St. Bernardine: having been left an orphan from early childhood, he was brought up in Siena in a deep and enlightened Christian faith, so that when he reached youth, he wished to dedicate himself completely to Jesus in religious and priestly life in order to devote himself essentially to making Christ the Friend and Redeemer known to the greatest number.

After becoming a priest in the order of St. Francis, for twelve years he wished to continue to study and collect biblical, theological, moral, ascetic and mystical material to be well prepared to carry out his mission as a preacher in a worthy and satisfactory way. In 1417, beginning from Genoa, he set out for his vast and intense work, travelling all over the North and center of Italy, proclaiming Christ's love to everyone with ardor and passion and spreading everywhere devotion to the name of Jesus, especially under the symbol "IHS": *Iesus Hominum Salvator*. St. Bernardine was a great lover of Jesus, and he spent his whole life making the divine Savior known and loved, as is shown by his sermons in Latin and in the vernacular which are still relevant today.

Beloved young people! Like young Bernardine, try to get to know Jesus in a true and comprehensive way! Deepen your knowledge of Him in order to become friends with Him! Only knowledge of Jesus can give you real joy, which is not selfish and superficial; it is knowledge of Jesus which ends loneliness, overcomes sadness and uncertainty, gives real meaning to life, curbs passions, exalts ideals, expands energies in charity, brings light in decisive choices. We read in the *Imitation of Christ* as follows: "When Jesus is present, everything is good and nothing seems difficult; when Jesus is absent, everything becomes heavy. When Jesus does not speak interiorly, consolation is of no avail; but if Jesus says only one word, great consolation is felt.... What can the world give you without Jesus? To be without Jesus is an unbearable hell, and to be with Jesus is a sweet paradise. If Jesus is with you there is no enemy who can harm you" (L. II, VIII, 1-2).

I repeat to you, too, what I said to the young people of Paris: "Jesus is not only a brother for us, a friend, a man of God. We recognize in Him the only Son of God, who is one with God the Father and whom the Father gave to the world.... Let Christ be for you the Way, the Truth, and the Life. Let Him be your salvation and your happiness. Let Him seize your whole life in order that it may reach all its dimensions with Him, that all your relationships, activities, feelings and thoughts may be integrated in Him, one could say 'Christified' " (June 1, 1980).

As St. Bernardine wished, let the name of Jesus be written in your thoughts, let it become a beating of your heart, let it spring honored and blessed from your lips: Jesus is the

Friend who does not betray, who loves you and wants your love! Let it be your firm resolution to get to know Him better and better by reading the Gospel, studying suitable works, reflecting on the biographies of the saints and on the experiences of converts.

Consistent in Faith

Learn next from St. Bernardine to live your Christian faith consistently. In fact, knowledge of Jesus is not enough; it is necessary to be consistent in life with the ideas professed.

That saint lived in a difficult and even disconcerting age: Italy was certainly Christian at that time, but in practice, unfortunately, people did not live Christian lives. They were troubled, stormy times, marked by restlessness and conflicts in civil life and also within the Church. Above all, there was a painful situation of social injustice, hatred and enmity between one family and another, between one city and another. St. Bernardine was not daunted by the times or by men: with an intelligent and wise spirit, he realized at once that it was necessary to overcome evil by sowing good, and he planned his preaching and his ministry as an unyielding and continuous struggle against sin, calling Christians, laymen and priests, the humble and the powerful, masters and workers, to consistency of life. His eloquence was lively and joyful, but also sharp and relentless, and with fearless courage he faced evil in every place, lashing out at vices and defects, without sparing anyone, exhorting to conversion and repentance, calling to forgiveness and peace. He knew how to be humorous and ironic when need be, and in his sermons he left us amusing and revealing sketches of the life of his time.

The humanist Maffeo Vegio, a contemporary of his, relates that the faithful approached the sacraments in such great numbers that sometimes there were not enough priests to hear confessions and administer the Eucharist.

And this, dear young people, is the second pressing exhortation: Be consistent! Christian faith, our own dignity and the expectation of the present-day world essentially need this commitment of consistency. And the first fundamental expression of consistency is the struggle against sin, that is, the constant and even heroic effort to live in grace. Unfortunately we live in an age in which sin has even become an industry, which produces money, inspires economic plans, bestows prosperity. This situation is certainly striking and terrible. Yet we must not let ourselves be frightened or oppressed. Any age demands "consistency" from the Christian. And so, even in present-day society, immersed in a lay and permissive atmosphere, which may tempt and entice you young people, remain consistent with the message and the friendship of Jesus; live in grace, abide in His love, putting into practice the whole moral law, nourishing your soul with the body of Christ, taking advantage of the sacrament of Penance periodically and seriously.

Finally, learn from St. Bernardine the courage of witness. He was, moreover, a resolute and fearless witness of Christ. In fact, even before, at the time of his adolescence, he had been an example among the young people of Siena, and in 1400, when the terrible plague broke out, with twelve other friends of his he was not afraid to devote himself to helping the poor sick, at the risk of his own life.

You, too, be courageous! The world needs convinced and fearless witnesses. It is not enough to discuss, it is necessary to act! Let your consistency become witness, and let the first form of this commitment be "availability." Always feel ready, like the Good Samaritan, to love, to assist, to help, in the family, at work, in recreation, with those who are near and those who are far away. Help your priests, too, in the various parish activities; help your bishops! Also consider, with seriousness and generosity, whether the Lord might not be also calling some of you to priestly, religious, and missionary life. Every year your seminary waits anxiously and confidently for someone to enter to begin the specific formation for the priesthood. In the world of today, hungry for Christ and His Gospel, your witness is needed!

Turn to the Virgin Mary

I conclude by entrusting you to the Virgin Mary, to whom St. Bernardine was extremely devoted and whom, it can be said, he went proclaiming all over Italy every day. Having lost his own mother, he chose our Lady as his mother and always lavished his affection on her and trusted completely in her. He became the singer of Mary's beauty, it can be affirmed, and preaching her mediation with inspired love, he was not afraid to state: "Every grace that is given to men proceeds from a triple ordained cause: from God it passes to Christ, from Christ it passes to the Virgin, from the Virgin it is given to us" *(Sermo* VI in festis B.V.M. De Annun. a. 1, c. 2).

Turn to her every day with confidence and with love, and ask her for the grace of the beauty of your soul and of your life, of what alone can make you happy.

With these wishes, invoking the intercession of St. Bernardine, I impart to you the apostolic blessing. May it always accompany you as a sign of my deepest affection.

Live Authentic Christian Lives

On September 3, 1980, the Holy Father met with the young members of the "Marian Association of Italy." He delivered the following message to them.

And now a kind greeting to all young people who, emulating their contemporaries present at the other audiences, have come to show their affection to the Pope, and to receive from him words of advice and encouragement. My special thought goes towards the numerous group of young people from the "Marian Association of Italy," guided by the Lazzarist Fathers, on the occasion of the sixtieth anniversary of the apparition of the most holy Virgin to St. Catherine Labouré.

Knowing well your generous availability, I wish to call to your attention the duty of an authentic Christian behavior in your lives. We should esteem them and possess them, because there is still something lacking. May the sincere love for God and the theological virtue of hope direct your steps towards gaining spiritual and eternal wealth. Consecrate all your energy towards these ideals, rejecting as contemptible to your baptismal dignity what has no reference to them. May my apostolic blessing, which I extend to all those dear to you, accompany you.

Live in Faith

The Holy Father addressed the following words of encouragement to the young pilgrims of Abbiategrasso on September 7, 1980.

Present here is a group of young people from Abbiate-grasso with their assistant, who are completing a singular pilgrimage, on foot, from the Abbey of Montecassino to their own city, on the occasion of the 15th centenary of the birth of St. Benedict.

Dearest young people, I wish to offer you the most heartfelt greeting and encouragement for a true walk of faith throughout your whole life, in harmonious union with the Benedictine ideal: prayer and work. So, for your happiness and your good! With my paternal blessing.

Be Loyal and Love the Church, Your Family and Your City

During his pastoral visit to Velletri, the Holy Father met with over three thousand young people in the Square of San Clemente on the evening of September 7, 1980. He offered them these encouraging words:

My dear young people!

My special cordial greetings to you! To you the expression of my heartfelt affection in the Lord!

In coming to this city of yours, I ardently wanted to meet you to show you in a special way the love the Pope and the whole Church feels for you. I am happy to see you and be able to speak to you; your presence brings me comfort and joy, and I thank you. Certainly, it would be lovely and consoling to be able to meet you individually; but that is not possible. This is the reason the Lord has entrusted you to your priests, who must be your guides, your friends, your confidants. All I can do is see you like this, all together at this lively and meaningful meeting, and greet you collectively in a spiritual way. But know that the Pope loves you, thinks of you and worries about you, would want you to be always good and happy, and for this intention he offers his prayers.

As you greet the Pope and sing hymns to him who has come in the name of Christ, I too raise my voice and shout: "Hurrah for the young, hurrah for all the youth of Velletri!"

On this special day I wish to leave with you a message which may be of help to you, and to all those who face life, as a program and directive for your choices.

Firm in Faith and Watchful

Remember first of all that you are part of a city, and hence of national and international society. Therefore, love this city of yours! Make it always more beautiful, welcoming, pleasant, joyous! Make it your business to be good citizens, responsible and worthy of your ancestors. Do not forget those who during World War II died or had to suffer so much for liberty and brotherhood! Contribute as much as possible to resolving the present problems of society by studying, working, having respect for old people and children, love for the suffering and ill, committing yourselves to improving the city in all its areas, and also with that sense of honesty, uprightness, and recognition that renders social life kind and serene. Loving your city in a concrete way, feeling yourselves to be living, conscious cells of this delicate and essential body of society, you will also succeed in truly loving your country and all of humanity.

Remember that you are a part of the local Church, and that means of your diocese and your individual parish and, through the local Church, you are a part of the universal Church. The city of Velletri in times past distinguished itself for its loyalty to the Christian religion and the Catholic Church. You too be loyal: Love the Church! Today, certainly, loyalty is more difficult, more heroic, and much more costly: Modern civilization is made up of models of behavior that do not always, or not completely, adhere to the message of Christ and the Church; rather, sometimes it decidedly battles it. Do not be disturbed! Do not be discouraged! The Word of God remains true for eternity; God is faithful (1 Cor. 1:9). Be firm in faith and be watchful (1 Pt. 5:8). Live your Baptism and Confirmation with the victorious serenity of those who appreciate the values you possess. Love your Church! Help the bishop, help the priests. Collaborate with them so that your city may always remain Christian and practicing. Show your faithfulness particularly by your participation in the Sunday and feast-day liturgy; do not ever miss Mass, and if possible, never fail to meet with Christ in Eucharistic Communion! Widen your gaze to the universal Church so that you are able to involve yourselves also in the great needs of the apostolate and of witness, ready to welcome the Lord's voice if He calls you to the priestly or religious life.

Love Your Family

Finally, remember that you are part of a family. Love your family! Love your parents and all those who love you! The family, as you know, is the historic and visible expression of the love of God, who in this way wished to make people capable of loving and giving their lives, precisely because they are created "in his image and likeness." It is sad to think that certain ideologies want to destroy the family, spreading alienation and causing disputes! It is distressing to think that so many young people leave their own homes, casting their parents into bitterness and despair! That is not the way, that is not the way. Love your families with generosity, patience, tact, tolerating those imperfections which are not lacking in any person whatsoever. Make your home an oasis of peace and confidence; pray with your families! And prepare yourselves also to form families of your own in the future: do it in such a way that your love will always remain pure and serene through intimate friendship with Jesus!

Dear young people, this is what I wanted to suggest to you in this meeting just for you alone! May the Madonna of Grace, especially venerated by you, help and protect you: offer your hearts and your youth to her!

Let my blessing help you, which I impart to you with affection, and which I extend with pleasure to all your dear ones.

You and I
Make Up the Church

The Holy Father met with the young people of Frascati in the sports arena of the Domus Iuventutis *Oratory at Capocroce, September 8, 1980. Following is the text of the talk that had been prepared, but not delivered, since the Pope spoke to the group extemporaneously.*

My very dear young people,

I am happy to be among you, dear young people of Frascati, members of the Diocesan Catechist Group, Catholic Action, and the GEN and Communion and Liberation movements. You are gathered here for what has become an habitual conversation with the Pope, accompanied by many other young people and representing as well so many boys and girls who work with you in the effort to build a living society, because you are animated by the love of Christ. And it is in the name and in the victorious sign of Christ that I today give my paternal and joyful greetings to each of you in this piazza that has become the garden of joyful hopes.

I thank you for this meeting which, as on every other occasion, holds a central place in my visit to the ecclesial community of Frascati, and which on today's occasion is animated also by your sincere and courageous involvement. I have, in fact, listened with great pleasure to the news you gave me about your commitment to know Christ and make Him known in the environment that surrounds you, by means of plans for ever renewed and updated evangelization, plans for new developments in Christian life on the various strata of social connections and valid contributions of concrete testimony of faith. Thanks, dear young ones, for everything you do, considering that you are offering a message of joy and trust to a society that is at times disheartened and deeply exasperated by its own internal contradictions. Yours is a grand mission that the Church desires to sustain, animate, and encourage in the name of the Gospel, which is Good News, and hence an announcement of salvation and everlasting happiness of heart.

To Learn the Art of Facing Challenges

The Church has the mandate, entrusted to the feeble efforts of men oftentimes fragile and imperfect, of authentically communicating Christ to you in His divine Word and in His life through the liturgy and the sacraments, so that you can assume your future responsibilities and your important decisions in the spirit and attitude of Christ. Thus, you will be able, in the accomplishment of your personal tasks, to be an influence also on the activities of others and on the hoped-for change in civilized society.

You are asked to learn the difficult and at the same time attractive art of facing the recurring challenges presented by daily worldly commitment, in the light of the cross and resurrection of Christ, in a giving that does not even exclude the total sacrifice of your own selves, and it is open, simultaneously and with certainty, to a bright dawn of renewal that cannot fail, because ours is a hope that does not disappoint (cf. Rom. 5:5).

As I said last October to 20,000 young people gathered in Madison Square Garden in New York: "When you are astonished at your own mystery, look to Christ who offers you the meaning of life. When you seek to know what being a mature person means, look to Christ who is the fullness of the human being. And when you try to imagine what will be your role in the future of the world...look to Christ. It is only in Christ that you will fully reach your potential both as men and women and as citizens" (Teaching of John Paul II, II-2, p. 567).

Part of the Church

While the Church has the task of instilling Christ in you so that you may arrive at the full maturity of man in Him who is the perfect Man and at the same time the Son of God, on your part, receiving His words of life, embody always deeper within yourselves the very mystery of the Church; come in and be a part of it, take on its future and destiny, and thus you will be called to render a service to the Church and at the same time to your brothers and sisters. You are in the most varied ways summoned, in harmony with the inner dispositions of your hearts, to serve in truth and in charity those who are still suffering because of the weakness and fatigue of their long, uncertain journey.

In this regard let us remember together what Jesus said during the Last Supper after the washing of the feet: "If I then, your Lord and Teacher, have washed your feet, you also ought to wash one another's feet. For I have given you an example, that you also should do as I have done to you" (Jn. 13:14-15). And St. Paul interpreted this mandate of Christ's with the words: "We who are strong ought to bear with the failings of the weak, and not to please ourselves....

Christ did not please himself" (Rom. 1:1-3). Dear young people, you and I and all of us together make up the Church, and we are called to "please our neighbor for his good, to edify him" (Rom. 15:20), offering to all "the surpassing worth of knowing Jesus Christ" (Phil. 3:8), in whom alone is true love for man and the fullness of life.

Accepting the Church

And now my invitation to look to Christ in order to render a service to your brothers takes on an exact meaning which I offer for your reflections: the Church needs you.

You are convinced of it. The Church expects much of you; in fact, it depends on your commitment in witnessing Christ and conveying the Gospel to others. You who are the "Church" cannot back away from such an appeal, justified by your Catholic training, to collaborate by every means in spreading the Gospel. This service is expected of you. But serving the Church means accepting its make-up, hierarchical and spiritual at the same time, and so to feel part of an ordered fabric, whose government is entrusted to the pastors whom Christ continually chooses as successors of the Apostles. There cannot exist true, effective, and lasting service without the unity of purpose and initiatives with the diocesan bishops so as to cooperate in pastoral work to the benefit of the entire ecclesial community.

This work imposes special priority choices, demands a coordinated development in time and place, must be defended from many dangers. All that requires vigilance, the protection and administration of the bishop, who must be given your trustful and obedient collaboration. You must serve the Church in the Church, in a communion of love and discipline with the legitimately constituted pastors.

Then there exists a very special service, which is that rendered by the ministerial priesthood, a sublime mission that assures the continuity among men of the redeeming work of Christ. The Church needs men who guarantee their own brothers a lifelong service, exceedingly high and exalting: that is, being stewards and administrators of God's mysteries, living instruments of forgiveness and grace, ministers of the Word that saves.

Dear young people, today Jesus Christ directs to you, through His Vicar, an appeal to follow Him with an irrevocable and total giving in order to be His living representatives and continuers of His redemptive ministry among the masses longing for salvation. It is an appeal made to your freedom and your generosity. I firmly hope the voice of Jesus penetrates your hearts, becomes one with the hopes, enlivens the interior views of the most generous among you. Your response to His invitation is not only a proof of human courage, but also and above all the genuine result of the effectiveness of divine grace.

It is, then, in prayer, meditation, and profound longing to cleave to Christ the Lord that you must agree with such an appeal by giving the Church, when the Lord calls, the sublime service of the ministerial priesthood.

May the most holy Virgin, Mother of the Church, whose birth we celebrate today, that is, the radiant and promising dawn of the great work of man's redemption, help you in your reflection, open your hearts to a genuine giving, and lend you the courage to take on with trust and gladness the fruitful responsibility of serving the Church.

May my affectionate blessing accompany you always.

Called To Discover Christian Joy

On September 14, 1980, Pope John Paul II met the young people of Siena and Tuscany and addressed them as follows.

My very dear young people of Siena and Tuscany,

I am happy to be with you in this magnificent square and under the splendid light that shines on us from the figure and teaching of the Sienese virgin, Catherine Benincasa, on the occasion of the sixth centenary of her most holy death.

I greet everybody with the most heartfelt feeling, that of a Father and Pastor, and I thank you warmly for participating in this meeting and for the sincere enthusiasm and the consolation you afford me in seeing you so full of life, exuberance, and joy.

Yes, joy! It is just this display of your spirit, summarizing and crowning all the others, that catches my attention and inspires this brief but cordial exhortation of mine in our joyous meeting of hearts. Christian joy, in fact, was the distinguishing mark of your great fellow-citizen, who even in the midst of innumerable tribulations and disappointments, succeeded in living it in such depth as to spill its sweetness over into every conversation and writing of hers. She wrote in a letter: "Take pleasure, and exult, and remain in the holy, sweet affection of God. Take pleasure in sweet labors" (cf. Letter 219). And in another: "Clothe yourselves in

Christ crucified, and inebriate yourselves in His blood: therein you will find happiness and perfect peace" (cf. Letter 187). She wrote to Daniela of Orvieto: "Every time is a time of love for the soul, and every place is a place of love for it: if it is in the time of penitence, this is the time of joyfulness and consolation for it, and if out of necessity or obedience it must leave, it takes equal pleasure" (cf. Letter 213).

Christian joy rises to such heights when a decisive road of faith is taken. You too, O Sienese youth, heirs of such a shining religious tradition, are called to the discovery or rediscovery of this joy, that is, of this Good News brought upon the earth by "sweet Jesus," as the saint called Him. Whether you place yourselves in contact with nature, whether you meet with others, you should always be aware of this profound reality that is the distinguishing mark of Christianity. But above all, in your encounters with God—the living God of Abraham, Isaac and Jacob, not the god of the philosophers—express to Him the Alleluia of paschal joy, the song of the redeemed, of the new covenant, of "brothers dwelling in unity" (cf. Ps. 132:1).

Young people of Siena and Tuscany, I say to you: Learn how to unite your efforts in order to assure this joy to yourselves and whomever you encounter on the path of your day, in the family, school, work, play. There are youths like yourselves who have not yet found it, there are busy men and women who do not have the time and spirit to seek it, there are sick people in the hospitals and old people in the homes who suffer from abandonment and loneliness: All these sisters and brothers await a smile from you, a word from you, your help, your friendship, and your handshake. Do not deny any one the joy that comes from such gestures: thus you will bring comfort to them together with benefit to yourselves, because, as Sacred Scripture says: "It is more blessed to give than to receive" (Acts 20:35).

From this way of living and working you will also derive that sense of optimism and trust which, although not denying the negative aspects that permeate our society, will cause you to reject all those disintegrating and sterile excesses which do not allow you to see the positive and beautiful sides of people and events. Certainly, it is the task of healthy psychology to train us to have such a serene outlook, but it is also an effect of the Spirit that so animated St. Catherine in her sweet but strong religious and social activity for the redemption of her time, tormented no less than our own. Let us call on that self-same Spirit whose fruit is "love, joy, peace..." (cf. Gal. 5:22), so that, as He granted Catherine each day the joy of living her particular vocation of mediator and peacemaker between the powers of her time, and of consoler of the poor and the afflicted, so He will grant you also the same vocation of workers for peace and bearers of the "Good News" to the world of to-day that looks to you and trusts in your sincerity, loyalty, and courage.

Dear young people, accept this trust that I place in your hands today, and put it into practice with all the enthusiasm you are capable of. Only thus will you succeed in dispelling the fears and uncertainties that lie heavy on the future, and you will be the heralds and bearers of a new civilization, of the New Covenant between God and man.

To that end may the special apostolic blessing that now, through the intercession of St. Catherine, I impart with all my heart to all of you and your friends, sustain and comfort you.

Jesus Christ Is the "Way, Truth, and Life"

The Holy Father's meeting with the young people of Cassino took place on Saturday afternoon, September 20, 1980. After listening to the greeting of the president of Catholic Action, Dr. D'Agostino, the Holy Father delivered the following address.

It is with sincere joy that I meet you, beloved young people of Cassino: The appointment with the young is always a specially welcome moment of my pastoral journeys and it has become a very fine and comforting custom. I would like to greet you individually, but time does not allow me to linger for long, and I must confine myself to a few words, which, however, I address to you from the bottom of my heart.

To Strengthen You in Hope

The president of Catholic Action in the diocese, expressing your sentiments, said that "the young desire words of certainty in the difficult path of life." Well, my deep desire is precisely to strengthen your faith and your hope. Man, in fact, can do without many things, but he cannot renounce those certainties which alone give his existence value and meaning. As you well know, certainty springs from the truth and the truth is such when it leads to life. Jesus Christ is precisely the Way that leads to the truth and

He is "true" because He is Life and gives life. All men are called to pass along this way; we are all pupils of this Master, who has words of eternal life.

The saints traveled this Way in an edifying manner, and today we remember them and venerate them as milestones, as signs set up for the People of God. St. Benedict, the fifteenth centenary of whose birth we are celebrating, was a "real man" because he was able to find in the search for God the meaning and the hope of his existence in the society of that historical moment in which one age was drawing to a close and another was being born. Right from his youth, he did not hesitate to make a courageous choice between the offerings of a prosperous and promising earthly life, and God's superior requirements.

In the history of mankind it has always happened that when God is forgotten, idols are fabricated in His stead: "Miserable, with their hopes set on dead things, are the men who give the name 'gods' to the works of men's hands" (Wis. 13:10). For man, if he trust in his own strength, is like a living person put in a condition of death, and the world can offer him only prospects of death: drugs, violence, terrorism, tyranny, consumerism of every kind. The opposite of all that is: life, love, peace, joy, truth, respect for man and for things, that is, all that is derived from faith in God and from Christian commitment.

It is about these values that you young people must make a pronouncement, and it is towards such choices that you must strain, with the enthusiasm and commitment characteristic of your age.

What God Wants

I am happy to recall to you, too, what I had occasion to say to the young people of France at my meeting with them: "Man cannot be happy except to the extent to which he is capable of accepting the requirements that his own humanity, his dignity as a man, impose upon him. The requirements that God imposes upon him.... Moral permissiveness does not make men happy. The consumer society does not make men happy. They have never done so" (Address to Youth, June 1, 1980, no. 8).

I am close to each and every one of you with great affection, so that you may be able to travel the one true way and choose the one certainty, which is Jesus Christ, man's Redeemer. He accompanies you so that you may live a truly human and Christian life. May you also be strengthened by my blessing, which I willingly extend to your families.

Raise a Joyful Song to Mary

On October 1, 1980, Pope John Paul II spoke to the young people present about the value of the holy rosary.

And now a fatherly and affectionate thought for you, dear young people.

I will take the opportunity of the feast of the Blessed Virgin, celebrated yesterday, but which in a way extends throughout the whole month of October. The holy rosary introduces us into the very heart of faith. With our thought fixed on it, we greet repeatedly, joyfully, the holy Mother of God; declare blessed the Son, the sweet fruit of her womb; and invoke her motherly protection in life and in death.

Dear young people, esteem the rosary, raise a joyful song to the Queen of heaven, and may you delight in reciting it.

The holy rosary, with its alternating verses of joy and sorrow, as well as of hope in the resurrection, may be of use to you too, dear sick people who are present, or who have remained at home. It shows, through the vicissitudes of the Son of God and of the Virgin, how constant in human life is the alternation of good and evil, calm and storms, joyful days and sad ones. Sorrow weighs on human nature, created for joy; but it is also a regenerating and sanctifying element, as we can see very well in the life of Christ and His Mother.

Remember the Real Priorities

On October 1, 1980, the Holy Father addressed the following message to the students of the North American College who had come to see the Pope.

On this first anniversary of my pastoral visit to the United States, I offer a word of special greeting to the new students at the North American College. Dear young men, you have come to Rome to prepare for the priesthood by growing in the knowledge and love of our Lord Jesus Christ. Never forget the real priorities of your vocation: You are called to *hear* and *guard* and *do* the Word of God, in order to be able to *proclaim* it faithfully and effectively. In this great task you will always be guided by the Magisterium of the Church, sustained by prayer, and assisted by the intercession and protection of our Blessed Mother Mary.

Integrate Physical Gifts with Spiritual Ones

On October 2, 1980, the Holy Father received in the Paul VI Hall the participants in the Twelfth Youth Games, organized by the Italian National Olympic Committee and the Minister of Public Instruction to promote sports activities for the youth of Italy. The following is the Pope's message to the more than five thousand young athletes.

Dear leaders of the sports federations belonging to C.O.N.I., Dear boys and girls!

This visit of yours, at the end of the national competitions of the Youth Games, which you have carried out in Rome during these days, is a particularly welcome one for me. I am happy to see you, to welcome you. I thank you for the delicate thought you had to come and greet the Pope before returning to your homes and to the regions of Italy from which you come and which you well represent. I express my gratitude in particular to Dr. Franco Carraro, the President of the Italian Olympic Committee, for the significant words that he wished to address to me now, on behalf of you all.

Your enthusiastic and joyful presence stirs up again in my heart so many dear memories linked with my previous pastoral experience in the midst of the young athletes of Poland.

You well know the esteem that the Church nourishes for you, and how Christian faith does not humiliate, but gives new value to, and ennobles sports in its various expressions.

You also know with what interest the Pope follows your sporting activities and with what satisfaction he looks to your athletic events, in which you show the uncommon gifts of fortitude, discipline and daring with which the Lord has adorned you. Your president now spoke about your training in "loyalty," "self-control," "courage," "generosity," "cooperation" and "brotherhood": well, are not these so many goals at which the Church aims in the education and advancement of youth? Are not these the deepest aspirations and requirements of the Gospel message?

In this connection, while I exhort you always to give the best of your energies and your abilities in peaceful sporting competitions, I remind you at the same time not to consider sports as an end in itself, but rather as a precious element that will help you to give your person that fullness which comes from the integration of physical gifts with spiritual ones. In a word, the body must be subordinated to the spirit, which gives light, breath and sprint to life, and which makes you good athletes, good citizens, and good Christians.

Beloved young people, today's meeting with you takes place at a particularly important moment for the life of the Church. As many of you know, numerous bishops, coming from every part of the world, have gathered in the Vatican to take part in the Fifth Assembly of the Synod of Bishops on the role of the Christian family in the modern world. It is, in fact, extremely urgent to restore to all Christian families that beauty, that charge of love, and all those virtues which were impressed on it by the Lord. The family must really be the very special training ground in which your spiritual, athletic and social ideals may find a favorable climate and the necessary impetus to carry them further and make them mature to fullness. You, too, make your contribution so that your family may become more and more a real school of spiritual power and training for great human and social conquests.

May you be assisted and stimulated in this by the apostolic blessing, which I gladly impart to you here present, to your local sports associations, to your dear ones, and to all those who belong to this National Olympic Committee, as a token of my special favor.

"Be Young People of True, Deep Christian Faith!"

On October 5, 1980, the Holy Father delivered the following talk to the youth of Apulia at Otranto. The young people gathered in the Piazzale degli Eroi represented ecclesiastical associations active in the area.

Beloved young people!

At the conclusion of this intense and splendid day of pilgrimage, which has brought me to your Otranto to venerate the Eight Hundred Martyrs on the fifth centenary of their testimony of faith and of blood; I meet you, who are and represent the future of your city, of your country, of the Church. You bear in your hearts, as a very precious heritage, the admirable example of those people of Otranto, who, on August 14, 1480—at the dawn of what is historically considered the "modern age"—preferred to sacrifice their very lives rather than renounce the Christian faith.

This is a shining and glorious page for the secular and religious history of Italy, but especially for the history of the pilgrim Church in this world, which must pay, through the centuries, her price of suffering and persecution to keep intact and immaculate her faithfulness to the Bridegroom, Christ, the Man-God, man's Redeemer and Liberator.

You, beloved young people, are legitimately proud of belonging to a generous, courageous and strong stock, which is happy to see itself reflected in those eight hundred inhabitants of Otranto who, after defending with all means the survival, the dignity, and the freedom of their beloved city and their homes, were also able to defend in a sublime way the treasure of faith, communicated to them in Baptism.

To Die for Christ

We cannot read today without intense emotion the accounts of the eyewitnesses of the dramatic episode: The citizens of Otranto, over fifteen years of age, were faced with the tremendous alternative: either to deny faith in Jesus Christ, or to die an atrocious death. Antonio Pezzulla, a cloth cutter, answered for everyone: "We believe in Jesus Christ, the Son of God; and for Jesus Christ we are ready to die!" And immediately afterwards, all the others, exhorting one another, confirmed: "We die for Jesus Christ, all of us; we die willingly, in order not to deny His holy faith!"

Were they, perhaps, deluded? Were they men outside their time? No, beloved young people! Those were men, real, strong, decided, consistent men, deeply rooted in their history; they were men who intensely loved their city; they were strongly bound to their families; among them there were young people, like you, and they longed, like you, for joy, happiness, and love; they dreamed of an honest and secure job, a holy home, a serene and tranquil life in the civil and religious community!

And they made their choice for Christ, with clarity and with firmness!

In five hundred years the history of the world has undergone many changes; but man, in his deepest interiority, has kept the same desires, the same ideals, the same demands; he has remained exposed to the same temptations, which—in the name of fashionable systems and ideologies, try to empty the meaning and the value of the religious deed and of Christian faith itself.

Before the suggestions of certain contemporary ideologies, which exalt and proclaim theoretical or practical atheism, I ask you, young people of Otranto and of Apulia: Are you ready to repeat, with full conviction and awareness, the words of the Blessed Martyrs: "We choose to die for Christ with any kind of death, rather than deny Him"?

Authentic Faith

The Blessed Martyrs have left us—and in particular they have left you—two fundamental orders: love of one's earthly country and authenticity of Christian faith.

The Christian loves his earthly country. Love of one's country is a Christian virtue; following the example of Christ, His first disciples always manifested sincere *pietas,* deep respect and a clear loyalty towards their earthly country, even when they were outraged and persecuted to the point of death by the civil authorities.

During the course of two millennia, Christians have made, and continue to make today, their contribution of work, dedication, sacrifice, preparation, and blood for the civil, social, and economic progress of their country!

The second order left to us by the Blessed Martyrs is authenticity of faith. The Christian must always be *consistent with his faith.* "Martyrdom"—Clemente Alessandrino wrote—"consists in bearing witness to God. But every soul that seeks knowledge of God with purity, and obeys God's commandments, is a martyr, both in life and in words. For, if it does not shed its blood, it pours out its faith, since for faith it separates from the body even before dying" *(Stromata,* 4, 4, 15: ed. Staehlin II, p. 255).

Be young people of faith! of true, deep Christian faith! My great Predecessor Paul VI, on October 30, 1968, after speaking on the authenticity of faith, recited a prayer of his "to obtain faith."

Keeping in mind that incisive and profound text, I express the wish that, following the example of the Blessed Martyrs of Otranto, your faith, O young people, may be certain, that is, founded on the Word of God, on deep knowledge of the Gospel message, and especially of the life, Person, and work of Christ; and also on the interior witness of the Holy Spirit.

May your faith be strong; may it not hesitate, not waver, before the doubts, the uncertainties which philosophical systems or fashionable movements would like to suggest to you; may it not descend to compromises with certain concepts which would like to present Christianity as a mere ideology of historical character, and therefore to be placed at the same level as so many others, now outdated.

May your faith be joyful, because it is based on awareness of possessing a divine gift. When you pray and dialogue with God and when you converse with men, manifest the joy of this enviable possession.

Let your faith be active, let it manifest itself and take on concrete shape in laborious and generous charity towards brothers, who live crushed in sorrow and in need; let it be manifested in your serene adherence to the teaching of the truth; let it be expressed in your availability for all apostolic initiatives, in which you are called upon to participate for the expansion and the building up of the kingdom of Christ!

Renewed Commitment

I entrust these thoughts of mine to the Blessed Martyrs whose intercession I invoke today, particularly for you young people, in order that, like them, you may be able to live with renewed commitment the requirements of Christ's message.

With my apostolic benediction.

Amen!

Modernness of St. Maria Goretti's Message

On October 18, 1980, the Holy Father received in audience about four thousand pilgrims and large numbers of young people of Catholic Action of the diocese of Senigallia, on the occasion of the ninetieth anniversary of the birth of St. Maria Goretti. The group was led by Bishop Odo Fusi Pecci of Senigallia. The Pope delivered the following address.

Dear brothers and sisters!

I express to you my satisfaction in welcoming your pilgrimage, which represents the whole Diocese of Senigallia, in this hall today. My cordial greeting goes first of all to your bishop and my confrere, who has led you to Rome to the Successor of Peter. And I greet all of you present, with particular reference to the numerous dear youngsters and to young parish catechists. My fatherly and affectionate welcome goes to everyone, in the certain hope that today's meeting will really be a favorable opportunity to renew our common faith in Christ the Lord and our mutual love, as the nearby tombs of the glorious Apostles urge us to do.

I know that the reason for your pilgrimage is the ninetieth anniversary of the birth of St. Maria Goretti, born in Corinaldo, a parish of your diocese, where she learned the basic elements of faith and had the first experiences of parish life, even if later she had to follow her family in its move to the Pontine countryside of Latium. You have intended to pay homage in this way to the extraordinary figure of a saint who, while on the one hand she is a cause of pride for your diocesan community, on the other hand she shines as an example of virtue which holds good for, and can be proposed to, the whole of society.

Maria Goretti, in fact, was a martyr of chastity, that is, of a specific virtuous moral behavior, which has always been highly honored in the history of Christianity, even if many attempts have been made against it to depreciate its value in our times as in others. Certainly, the message that comes from the story of Maria Goretti is not of Manichaean order, of disparagement of the body and of sexuality, since a whole deep and sound theology of the body is characteristic of the biblical revelation. It is rather a question of a message concerning both personal dignity at the simple human level, which must be defended from all abuse and all violence, and the consecration of one's own energies, even physical ones, to the Lord and to the Church, in radical obedience to the law of God. The Christian does not cultivate chastity or any other virtue only for its own sake, making it an isolated purpose or an absolute ideal. St. Paul warns us: "If I deliver my body to be burned, and have not love, I gain nothing" (1 Cor. 13:3). Chastity is a very noble value, if it is ordained to Christ the Lord and integrated into the whole context of typical Christian life, on which the Holy Spirit confers its own fundamental and unmistakable tone, having among its fruits also "self-control" (Gal. 5:22), preceded and surrounded by many others.

Therefore, the invitation that comes from Maria Goretti to us all, and in particular to boys and girls, is to care for our own baptismal identity in depth, and to insert into the framework of this formation, as one of its elements, also the thorough and jealous cultivation of our own total dignity, not only Christian but also human, of which chastity is an expression of prime importance.

In this sense, dear brothers and sisters, you have nothing else to do but continue and intensify all the activities of diocesan life which already distinguish you. I am informed, in fact, that Catholic Action for the young is flourishing among you, with its various and fruitful pedagogical initiatives, which foster community experiences of joy and commitment, and prepare for a life of both ecclesial and civil responsibility.

A decisive area, to which you give your care, is also that of catechists. I wish to remind them of the extreme seriousness of this role, such a determining one for the growth of the young in faith. Everything that is done for catechists and by catechists is certainly worthy of the choicest graces and heavenly rewards. Maria Goretti's strength certainly had its roots also in that catechetical teaching which she had the fortune to receive in her own family.

And to you parents, and not only those present, there goes my urgent and encouraging invitation to dedicate your Christian intelligence to your family and children. Maria Goretti, who left Corinaldo illiterate, found the best school precisely in her father and mother, since they had been formed by assiduous participation in parish catechesis and in the liturgical life of their birthplace. It is an example which fits well into the framework of the present Synod of Bishops, which in these very days is studying the various aspects and problems of the family in the modern world.

I am happy, therefore, to wish all of you all happiness in the Lord, assuring you that I will remember you in prayer to Him, so that "speaking the truth in love, we... grow up in every way into him who is the Head" (Eph. 4:15). May He always accompany you with His grace, of which my apostolic blessing, which I willingly impart to all of you and extend to your dear ones and to the whole beloved Diocese of Senigallia, is intended to be a token.

"The Church Relies a Great Deal on You"

At the general audience on October 27, 1980, the Holy Father addressed these beautiful words of encouragement to the young people present.

I greet all the dear young people present here and assure them of my special affection. I call upon you always to be strong and joyful witnesses to your faith in Christ, whom the world of today needs so much. Always be proud of your Christian identity, which you must discover more and more, and the whole Church will be proud of you; she relies a great deal, in fact, both on your enthusiasm and on your sense of responsibility for the building of a more radiant future. Therefore, I bless you willingly.

"Hail Mary"

On October 29, 1980, the Holy Father addressed the young people present at the general audience with the following words.

Still feeling the intense joy caused last Sunday by the solemn ceremony of three beatifications, while I extend to you, beloved young people, my special greeting, I repeat to you some words that Don Luigi Orione wrote to his young followers: "I pray humbly but with filial confidence to the Blessed Virgin so that she may assist you and comfort you, so that she may save you from discouragement..." (Letter of August 21, 1939). And on another occasion he exclaimed: "Oh young people! Hail Mary, always!... Hail Mary, and forward!... Hail Mary, until blessed Paradise!" (Writing of May, 1923)

I, too, willingly leave you this exhortation and this program of life together with my blessing.

Advance in the Way
of Dedication

Recorded December 9, 1980 is the Holy Father's "special" message to the young.

My attention now goes to all the young people present, and, in particular, to the students who have been awarded the title "Ensigns of Work" for the moral and intellectual qualities shown during the course of their studies. Beloved in Christ, may the significant award in recognition of your commitment during these years, be for you an incentive to advance consistently along the way of generous dedication to duty, which faith validly enlightens and guides. Addressing also a special thought to the "Volunteers of the Focolari Movement," who have in these days taken part in a meeting at the Mariapolis center at Rocca di Papa, I willingly bless you all.

Open Your Hearts
to Christ

The first event on the Pope's last day of his pilgrimage in Germany, November 19, 1980, was a Mass for youth celebrated in Munich's "There-sienwiese." The Holy Father delivered the following homily.

Dear brothers and sisters,
Dear young people,

When Christ speaks about the kingdom of God He often uses images and parables. His image of the "harvest," of the "great harvest," necessarily reminded His listeners of that annually recurring and so very much longed-for time when people could finally begin to harvest the fruit that had grown at the cost of considerable human effort.

The parable of the "harvest" today sends our thoughts in the same direction, although, as people from highly industrialized countries, we can hardly imagine any more what the ripening and harvesting of the fruits of the earth once meant for the farmer and people in general.

With the image of grain ripening for harvest, Christ wants to indicate *the inner growth and maturation of man.*

Man is bound by and dependent upon his own nature. At the same time, he towers above it with the inner nature of his personal being. Thus, *human maturation is something different* from the ripening of the fruits of nature. This does not involve only physical and intellectual effort. An important part of the maturation process in man involves the spiritual, the religious dimension of his being. When Christ speaks of the "harvest" He means that man must mature towards God and then *in God* Himself; in His kingdom, he will receive the fruit of his effort and maturation.

I would like to point out this truth of the Gospel to you young people of today, both with great seriousness and at the same time with cheerful hope. You have arrived at a particularly important and critical time in your lives, in which much, or perhaps even everything, that will determine your further development and your future, will be decided.

The knowledge of the truth is of basic importance for the formation of one's personality and for the building of the inner human being. Man can *only* be truly mature *with the truth and in the truth.* In this lies the profound meaning and importance of education which the entire educational system from the schools to the universities must serve. They must help young people to know and understand the world and themselves; they must help them to see what gives the existence and the works of man in the world their full meaning. For that reason, education must also help them to know God. Man cannot live without knowing *the significance of this existence.*

Strength To Build a More Human World

This search, finding of directions, and maturing with the basic and full truth of reality is, however, not easy. It has always been necessary to overcome numerous difficulties. It is apparently this problem that St. Paul refers to when he writes in his Second Epistle to the Thessalonians: "We beg you...not to be quickly shaken in mind or excited.... Let no one deceive you in any way...!" (2 Thes. 2:1-3) These words, addressed to a new group of the earliest Christians, must be reread today against the different background of our modern civilization and culture. Thus, I would like to call out to you young people of today: Do not be discouraged! Do not be deceived!

Be thankful if you have good parents who encourage and direct you onto the right path. Perhaps there are more of them than you can recognize at first sight. However, many young people suffer from their parents, feel that their parents do not understand them, or even abandon them. Others have to find the path to faith without, or even against, the will of their parents. Many suffer as a result of the "achievement pressures" in the schools, and encounter insecurity with respect to the prospects for a professional future. Should one not be afraid that technical and economic development will destroy man's natural living conditions? And anyway, what will be the future of our world which is divided into military power blocs, poor and rich nations, free and totalitarian states? Again and again wars flare up in this or that part of the world, causing death and misery to men. And then in many parts of the world, near and far, acts of the rawest kind of violence and bloody terror are carried out. Even here, where we commemorate before God the victims who were recently injured or suddenly killed on the edge of this large square by an explosive charge. It is hard to understand what man is capable of doing in the confusion of his mind and his heart.

It is against this background that we hear the call of the Gospel: "We beg you...not to be quickly shaken in mind or excited...!" All of these troubles and difficulties are part of the resistance with which we must nurture and test our growth in the fundamental truth. From this we derive the strength to help build a more just and more human world; from it we derive the readiness and courage to assume a growing measure of responsibility in the life of our society, state and Church. There is truly great consolation in the fact that, despite many shadows and darkness, there is a lot of good. The fact that too little is said of it does not mean that it is not there. Often one has to want to discover and recognize the good that is hidden. But it is at work and will perhaps at some later time become radiantly visible. Think, for example, what Mother Teresa of Calcutta had to do anonymously before a surprised world became aware of her work. Thus, I beg you not to be quickly shaken in mind or excited!

Temptations To Fall Away from the Faith

However, is it not the case that in your society, as you experience it in your surroundings, not a few who believe in Christ have become uncertain, or have lost their sense of orientation? And does that not have a particularly negative effect on young people? Does this not reveal something of the numerous temptations to fall away from the faith, of which the Apostle speaks in this Epistle?

The Word of God in today's liturgy gives us an idea of the *broad scope* of the loss of religious belief, such as seems to be emerging in our century, and makes its *dimensions* clear.

St. Paul writes: "For the mystery of lawlessness is already at work..." (2 Thes. 2:7). Would we not have to say that for our time as well? The *mystery of lawlessness,* falling away from God, has an inner structure and a definite dynamic gradation in the words of the Epistle of St. Paul: "...the man of lawlessness is revealed..., who opposes and exalts himself against every so-called god or object of worship so that he takes his seat in the temple of God proclaiming himself to be God" (2 Thes. 2:3-4). Thus, we have here an inner structure of negation, an uprooting of God in the heart of man and an uprooting of God in human society, with the aim, it is maintained, of obtaining a fuller "humanization" of man, i.e., making man human in a fuller sense of the word and in a certain way putting him in God's place, "deifying" him, as it were. This structure is very old and known to us from the first chapters of Genesis, i.e., the temptation of replacing the "divinity" (of the image and likeness of God), given to man by the Creator, with the "deification" of man against God, and without God, as is becoming visible under the atheistic conditions of many systems today.

Anyone who denies the fundamental truth of reality, who makes himself the measure of all things and, in doing so, puts himself in God's place; anyone who more or less consciously feels he can get along without God, the Creator of the world, without Christ, the Redeemer of man; anyone who, instead of seeking God, pursues idols, has always been fleeing from the sole, fundamental and saving truth.

There is also the attempt to escape by withdrawing into oneself. This can lead to giving up, "Nothing matters anyway." If the disciples of Jesus had acted in this way, the world would never have heard anything of the redeeming Gospel of Christ. Withdrawing into oneself can assume the form of attempting to bring about an expansion of consciousness. Not a few young people here in your country are in the process of destroying their inner beings by withdrawing into themselves with the aid of alcohol and drugs. Very often anxiety and despair are the reasons behind this, but often, too, it is based on a thirst for pleasure, a lack of asceticism, or the irresponsible curiosity of wanting to "try out" everything once. Withdrawing into oneself can also lead to pseudo-religious sects, which abuse your idealism and your enthusiasm and deprive you of the freedom of thought and conscience. This also includes the attempt to escape through doctrines of salvation that pretend to be able to attain true happiness on the basis of certain external practices, but which, in the final analysis, throw the affected person back on himself and the unsolved problem of loneliness.

Then there is the attempt to flee from the fundamental truth by moving outwards, away from oneself, i.e., into political and social utopias, idealized dreams of society. As necessary as ideals and aims are, utopian "magic formulae" will not get us anywhere, since they are usually accompanied by totalitarian power or the destructive use of violence.

The Good Shepherd Leads in Truth

You can see all this happening, the numerous escape routes people take to flee from the truth, the mysterious power of evil and iniquity that is at work. Are you never *confronted with the temptations of isolation and despondency?* There is an answer to this question in today's reading from the prophet Ezekiel. He speaks of a shepherd who follows his lost sheep into the wilderness in order to "rescue them from all places where they have been scattered on a day of clouds and thick darkness" (Ez. 34:12).

The *Shepherd who gathers up man on the dark path of his loneliness and disorientation and leads him back into the light is Christ.* He is the Good Shepherd. He is ever present in the hidden place of the "mystery of iniquity" and Himself takes charge of the important matter of human existence on this earth. He does it in truth by freeing *the heart of man from the fundamental contradiction* contained in wanting to deify man without or against God, which creates a climate of isolation and disorientation. On the path leading out of the darkness of loneliness to true humanity, Christ, the Good Shepherd, in profound, pursuing and accompanying love, takes charge of every individual person, in particular every young person.

The prophet Ezekiel goes on to say of the Shepherd: "And I will bring them out from the peoples and gather them from the countries and will bring them into their own land: And I will feed them on the mountains of Israel, by the fountains and in all the inhabited places of the country" (Ez. 34:13). "I will seek the lost, and I will bring back the crippled, and I will strengthen the weak, and the fat and the strong I will watch over; I will feed them in justice" (Ez. 34:16).

In this way Christ wants to accompany the *maturing of man* in his humanity. He accompanies, nurtures and strengthens us in the life of His Church with His Word and in His sacraments, with the body and blood of His Passover Feast. He nurtures us as the immortal *Son of God,* lets man partake of His divine Sonship, "deifies" him within, so that he will become "human" in the full sense of the word, so that man, created in the image and likeness of God, will attain his maturity in God.

You Are Called by God

For this reason Christ says the harvest is "great." It is great because of the immeasurable destiny of man. It is great because of the dignity of man. It is great in accordance with his calling. This wonderful harvest of the kingdom of God in humanity, the harvest of salvation in the history of man, peoples and nations is great. It is truly great, "but the laborers are few" (Mt. 9:37).

What does this mean? What is meant, dear young people, is that you have been called, called by God. My life, my human life is only meaningful, if I have been called by God in an important, decisive, final call. Only God can call man this way, no one but He. And this call of God constantly goes out, in and through Christ, to each and every one of you: To be workers in the harvest of your own humanity, workers in the vineyards of the Lord, in the Messianic harvest of humanity.

Jesus is in need of young people from your ranks who will follow His call and live as He did, poor and celibate, in order to be a living sign of the reality of God among your brothers and sisters.

God needs priests who will let themselves be led by the Good Shepherd into the service of His Word and His sacraments for men.

He needs people for the Catholic orders, men and women who will abandon everything in order to follow Him and in this way serve man.

He needs Christian married couples who will render to each other and to their children service leading to full maturation of humanity in God.

God needs people who are ready to help and to serve the poor, the sick, the abandoned, the afflicted and spiritually wounded.

Four Great Figures

The glorious, more-than-1000-year history of the Christian faith among your people is rich in individuals whose examples can provide an incentive in the fulfillment of your great calling. I would like to mention only four figures that come to me as a result of the present day and the city of Munich. There is St. Korbinian in the initial stages of the history of your faith in Christ, whose episcopal work laid the foundation for the Archdiocese of Munich-Freising. We are commemorating him in today's liturgy. There is the sainted Bishop Benno von Meissen, whose remains were laid to rest in Munich's *Frauenkirche*. He was a man of peace and reconciliation who preached non-violence in his time, a friend of the poor and the distressed. In connection with the present day, St. Elizabeth comes to mind, whose motto was: "Love, according to the Gospel." As the Princess of Wartburg she renounced all the privileges of her estate and devoted her life completely to the poor and the outcast. Finally, I would like to point out a man whom many of you or your parents knew personally, the Jesuit Father Rupert Mayer, at whose grave in the center of Munich, in the crypt of the *Bürgersaal,* many hundreds of people pause for a brief prayer every day. Despite the after-effects of severe wounds he suffered on a patrol mission in the First World War, he openly and undauntedly stood up for the rights of the Church and for freedom at a difficult time in history, and as a result, had to suffer the hardships of a concentration camp and exile.

Dear young people! Open your hearts to Christ's call! Your human life is a "unique adventure and enterprise," that can turn into both "a blessing and a curse." In view of you young people, who are the great hope of our future, let us ask the "Lord of the harvest" to send every one of you, and every one of your young fellow men on this earth, as laborers to His "great harvest," in keeping with the great wealth of callings and gifts in His kingdom on this earth.

I would like to close with a special blessing for our Evangelical Lutheran brothers and sisters, who today in this country are celebrating their *Day of Repentance and Prayer.* This day is dominated for them by a knowledge of the necessity for constant renewal and by the calling of the Church to commemorate our communion as a people and as a State before God in prayer. The Roman Catholic Church is united with you in this matter. Please include your Catholic fellow-citizens, as well as your brother, John Paul, and his ministry in your prayers this day. Amen.

INDEX

ALSO BY POPE JOHN PAUL II:

U.S.A.—THE MESSAGE OF JUSTICE, PEACE AND LOVE

Complete collection of the talks given by His Holiness, Pope John Paul II, during his historic visit to America, October 1-7, 1979: Boston, New York, Philadelphia, Des Moines, Chicago, Washington. What did the Vicar of Christ tell America wherever he went? A book to treasure, to meditate, to live by. 320 pages; cloth $5.95; paper $4.95 — EP1095

"YOU ARE THE FUTURE YOU ARE MY HOPE"

Talks of John Paul II **to young people** of all ages, from his papal election to the present. Reveals the stirring personal appeal of the Pope to the new generation. Excellent for youth and those involved in guidance. 326 pages, 16 pages of full-color photos; cloth $4.95; paper $3.95 — EP1120

POPE JOHN PAUL II—HE CAME TO US AS A FATHER

A **pictorial volume** in full color. Covers the entire visit of the Holy Father to the United States, from arrival through tour, to departure. A unique book on a unique historical event. A book of memories which, while recalling happy events, fosters spiritual renewal. 256 pages, over 300 full-color photographs, 100 black and white; gift edition $14.95— EP0957

Cassettes...

Boston, October 1, 1979

Welcome, Logan Airport; To Priests, Holy Cross Cathedral; Homily, Boston Common. 60 min. $4.95 — CSM0310

New York, October 2, 1979

Welcome, LaGuardia Airport; To International and Non-governmental Organizations, UN; To journalists,

UN; To UN staff members; Farewell message to UN.
36 min., $4.50 — CSM2642

Address of His Holiness, Pope John Paul II, to the United Nations

60 min., $4.95 — CSM0030

New York, October 2, 1979

Welcome, St. Patrick's Cathedral; Homily, Yankee Stadium. 35 min., $4.50 — CSM2640

New York, October 2, 1979

Address, Harlem; Address, South Bronx (Spanish). 15 min., $4.00 — CSM2643

New York, October 3, 1979

Homily, Morning Prayer, St. Patrick's Cathedral; To Youth, Madison Square Garden; Address, Battery Park; Address, Shea Stadium. 28 min., $4.25 — CSM2641

Philadelphia, October 3, 1979

Welcome, Cathedral Basilica of Sts. Peter and Paul; Homily, Logan Circle. 40 min., $4.50 — CSM3050

Philadelphia, October 4, 1979

Address, Immaculate Conception; Ukrainian Cathedral. 15 min., $4.00 — CSM3051

Philadelphia, October 4, 1979

Homily, Civic Center. 36 min., $4.50 — CSM3052

Des Moines, October 4, 1979

Homily, Living History Farms. 30 min., $4.25 — CSM0630

Chicago, October 4, 1979

To religious brothers. 20 min., $4.00 — CSM0430 ▶

Chicago, October 5, 1979
Homily, Grant Park. 30 min., $4.25 — CSM0431

Washington, D.C., October 6, 1979
Addresses of the President and the Pope at the White House. 40 min., $4.50 — CSM4110

Washington, D.C., October 6, 1979
Address to Organization of American States (Spanish and English). 30 min., $4.25 — CSM4111

Washington, D.C., October 7, 1979
To Women Religious, Shrine of the Immaculate Conception. 40 min., $4.50 — CSM3775

Washington, D.C., October 7, 1979
To Students, outside the Shrine of the Immaculate Conception; To Theologians and Catholic Educators, Catholic University of America. 25 min., $4.25 — CSM3770

Washington, D.C., October 7, 1979
Homily, Capitol Mall. 30 min., $4.25 — CSM1510

---

for the very young...   "YOU ARE MY FAVORITES"

Pope John Paul II to Children
Edited by the Daughters of St. Paul

In this colorful book, full of pictures and photographs, the Pope speaks to all the children of the world. He tells them about Jesus, faith, love, truth, school, holidays, sports, the Gospel, and much, much more. 192 pages; cloth $6.95 — EP1125

Daughters of St. Paul

IN MASSACHUSETTS
  50 St. Paul's Ave. Jamaica Plain, Boston, MA 02130;
    617-522-8911; 617-522-0875;
  172 Tremont Street, Boston, MA 02111; **617-426-5464;**
    617-426-4230
IN NEW YORK
  78 Fort Place, Staten Island, NY 10301; **212-447-5071**
  59 East 43rd Street, New York, NY 10017; **212-986-7580**
  7 State Street, New York, NY 10004; **212-447-5071**
  625 East 187th Street, Bronx, NY 10458; **212-584-0440**
  525 Main Street, Buffalo, NY 14203; **716-847-6044**
IN NEW JERSEY
  Hudson Mall — Route 440 and Communipaw Ave.,
    Jersey City, NJ 07304; **201-433-7740**
IN CONNECTICUT
  202 Fairfield Ave., Bridgeport, CT 06604; **203-335-9913**
IN OHIO
  2105 Ontario St. (at Prospect Ave.), Cleveland, OH 44115; **216-621-9427**
  25 E. Eighth Street, Cincinnati, OH 45202; **513-721-4838**
IN PENNSYLVANIA
  1719 Chestnut Street, Philadelphia, PA 19103; **215-568-2638**
IN FLORIDA
  2700 Biscayne Blvd., Miami, FL 33137; **305-573-1618**
IN LOUISIANA
  4403 Veterans Memorial Blvd., Metairie, LA 70002; **504-887-7631;**
    504-887-0113
  1800 South Acadian Thruway, P.O. Box 2028, Baton Rouge, LA 70821
    504-343-4057; 504-343-3814
IN MISSOURI
  1001 Pine Street (at North 10th), St. Louis, MO 63101; **314-621-0346;**
    314-231-1034
IN ILLINOIS
  172 North Michigan Ave., Chicago, IL 60601; **312-346-4228;**
    312-346-3240
IN TEXAS
  114 Main Plaza, San Antonio, TX 78205; **512-224-8101**
IN CALIFORNIA
  1570 Fifth Avenue, San Diego, CA 92101; **714-232-1442**
  46 Geary Street, San Francisco, CA 94108; **415-781-5180**
IN HAWAII
  1143 Bishop Street, Honolulu, HI 96813; **808-521-2731**
IN ALASKA
  750 West 5th Avenue, Anchorage AK 99501; **907-272-8183**
IN CANADA
  3022 Dufferin Street, Toronto 395, Ontario, Canada
IN ENGLAND
  128, Notting Hill Gate, London W11 3QG, England
  133 Corporation Street, Birmingham B4 6PH, England
  5A-7 Royal Exchange Square, Glasgow G1 3AH, England
  82 Bold Street, Liverpool L1 4HR, England
IN AUSTRALIA
  58 Abbotsford Rd., Homebush, N.S.W., Sydney 2140, Australia